THE
PSALMS

THE
PSALMS

A Guide for the
Heart and Soul

RABBI ALLAN L. BERKOWITZ

Epigraph Books
Rhinebeck, New York

Paperback ISBN 978-1-960090-18-8
eBook ISBN 978-1-960090-19-5

Library of Congress Control Number 2023911365

Cover design and interior art by Elie Berkowitz
Layout by Colin Rolfe

Epigraph Books
22 East Market Street, Suite 304
Rhinebeck, New York 12572
(845) 876-4861
epigraphps.com

For Nissan ben Avraham, of blessed memory

Dad: You lived your life filled with curiosity.
There were endless things to learn, and even
if they had no practical application, you found
them fascinating and worthy of exploration
(you knew the speed at which hummingbirds
flapped their wings and you were fascinated
by the outsized influence of the Hittites on
ancient Near Eastern civilizations). There are
many days I find myself reading something
fascinating, yet obscure, and those times
remind me that curiosity is wonderful and a
great gift I inherited from you.

CONTENTS

Introduction

FROM KING DAVID TO YOU, A JOURNEY OF THE HEART AND SOUL

According to Jewish tradition, King David authored the Psalms. That tradition tells us the one hundred and fifty Psalms were written over a lifetime by a poetic soul progressing through the ages and stages of his life. The young David, a shepherd wandering the hills above Jerusalem, composed poems reflecting his youthful optimism. The mature adult David crafted Psalms that are deep theological statements of faith. And with the wisdom, and sometimes jaded world view that comes with old age, the elderly David gave voice to the questions so many of us ponder: What is the true purpose of my life? How much suffering is too much, God? From where will I gain the strength to endure life's turmoil?

In between that youthful optimism and the bittersweet reflections of older age, David as King turned to God for strategic guidance; praised God for God's love and support of the Jewish people; and, not infrequently, did he recognize and thank God for his personal salvation (something that David was often in need of).

Like David, we experience moments of extreme optimism and appreciation when life is wondrous and great. We, too, know that life can be painful and threatening. And we are calmed by poems that give voice to our fears when words fail us. David knew—as we know—that to be human is to suffer moments of doubt and fear. When we experience challenge after challenge, at those periods when nothing we do seems to alter the downward trajectory, we also wonder when and from where shall relief finally come?

To live the life of a human being is to travel the narrative arc of youthful optimism, to search for salvation that gets us out of the troubles we may cause ourselves, and to question life's purpose with jaded eyes. To live life is to experience every emotion possible. And the Psalms are a gift that help us navigate those emotions and guide us through those peak experiences. David's questions give voice to our questions. David's poetic words answer the questions that are deep within our own souls.

The beauty and the importance of the Psalms is their collective ability to give voice at those moments when we are at a loss for words. When we are distraught outside the hospital room of a loved one whose diagnosis is devastating, it is Psalm 13 that so perfectly captures the depth of our despair:

> How long will my mind be overwhelmed, my
> heart consumed by grief all day?

When we have successfully come through a journey that threatened to take us down—extreme financial woes, or the demons of alcohol or drugs—the words from Psalm 121 release the unbridled joy and relief we feel at again seeing life on the other side of our personal chasm:

> I turn my eyes to the mountains; from where
> will my help come? My help is from God.

Like a flock of sheep lovingly nurtured by the shepherd who firmly redirects them when they threaten to go astray, and protects them when attacked, we are nurtured, sated, and protected by the eternal words of the Psalms.

About this Book

The Psalms are central to Jewish life. There isn't a prayer service in our Jewish ritual calendar that doesn't rely on the Psalms. For centuries, pious Jews have heeded our tradition's call to recite Psalms in times of trouble. There are Psalms of thanksgiving–everyone *should* give thanks on a regular basis. There are Psalms of joy–we all can benefit from recognizing the joy in our lives. There are Psalms that pick us up when we fall ill, are overwhelmed, lonely, confused. Indeed, every human emotion is captured somewhere in the Book of Psalms.

The Psalms: A Guide for the Heart and Soul is a directional arrow guiding you to and through many of the great Psalms. Here you will find the tools to easily access and understand them. You will discover words of life wisdom and insights into the human condition–both David's and yours. And you will encounter questions for your soul to ponder, mindfulness exercises, and suggestions for bringing the soulful messages of these Psalms into your daily life. You might embrace the reflections of Psalm 23 while visiting the gravesite of a loved one. You may choose to engage your children in a lesson of gratitude through a fun art project inspired by Psalm 67. In short, by learning how to enter the Psalms, you will discover how the Psalms will enter and touch your heart and soul.

For each Psalm in the book you will find:

- A comprehensive overview that makes the Psalm immediately accessible by summing up its themes, explaining the context within which it was written, and highlighting how universal and timeless are its reflections.

- Each overview concludes with a few select elements in the Psalm through which you will engage more deeply with the text. They focus on specific words or verses in the Psalm, often placing the spotlight on references that will better connect you to the Psalm; its role in Jewish life; and sometimes highlighting hidden treasures within the text (did you know there are fun word games and even artwork embedded in some Psalms?).

- "Soul Steps": Here you will find mindfulness exercises, questions to heighten your spiritual senses, and suggestions for bringing the Psalm into your own life in creative and spiritually uplifting ways.

In addition, you will find a series of insights to the collection of Psalms as a whole. These brief interludes place the Psalms in context: authorship, biographical insights to King David, the music of the Great Temple, even a fun and fascinating look at embedded mysteries within the Psalms. Through them the reader will gain a clearer understanding of the literature, history, and authorship behind the Psalms.

In Appendices A and B readers will find two charts—Psalms for Life's Moments. The charts, organized both numerically and topically, identify specific life experiences and suggest Psalms that speak to these moments, such as celebration of life, confronting life's challenges, needing God's support, honoring a special person, and so on. At these times, the reader can be guided to specific Psalms that might add poignancy to the moment, inspire reflection, or simply soothe a stirred soul.

The Authorship of the Psalms

I noted above that Jewish tradition considers David to have written the Psalms. Biblical scholarship, however, tells us that some of the Psalms were written by David, but many of them were not. Some Psalms were likely penned at a later date by unknown poets. In this book it would be too cumbersome to reference the authorship question each time I refer to the poet. And so, I use the name "David" as a general reference to the author of a particular Psalm. In doing so, I am suggesting that whether it was David or a later poet, in both cases, we inherit texts that hold the reflections of a deeply sensitive soul, an expert observer of the human condition, and a writer who was so very skillful in communicating about both life and our emotions.

Who Should Read this Book?

Many readers will find the Psalms are made accessible and highly readable. Their insights into the human condition are elucidated, and the guiding questions and mindfulness exercises will help you connect to the Psalms as a way to spiritually uplift your soul. For example, when you learn that Psalm 23 speaks of God's closeness and yet barely mentions God, it pushes us to ask ourselves, *Are there times when we feel the quiet presence of God?* There are questions for reflection to bring to your *Shabbat* or *Seder* dinner table. There are activities to guide children to better connect to some of the Psalms' life lessons.

Clergy, chaplains, and other helping professions will find that this book makes the Psalms quickly accessible and easily understood. It will be an invaluable resource as you nurture your constituents who are confronting peak emotional life experiences. And this book can be used as the textbook for an adult education class on the Psalms.

All of us can benefit from these beautiful poems that provide inspiration and speak to our aspirations. No matter what we may experience in life, there is a Psalm that speaks to it and gives voice to our emotions. This book will open a window into the beautiful words of the Psalms, that speak to our humanity and to our human condition. It is my hope that you will connect to them personally, deeply, and spiritually.

On Translation and Non-Gendered Language

The texts of the Psalms used in this book are based on the new Jewish Publication Society translation, with my own modifications so that the texts read in a comfortable, modern style while remaining as true to the original Hebrew as any translation can be.

Generally, I am sensitive to presenting references to God in a non-gendered form, preferring "God" instead of "He." And when possible, I avoid referring to God as "Lord" because of its gendered connotation. Two exceptions were necessary, both regarding Psalm 23, which presents unique challenges. Because Psalm 23 is so universally recognized by its famous opening line—*The Lord is my shepherd*—I have chosen to retain this reference to "Lord," though I am mindful it is uncomfortable for some readers.

Psalm 23 presents an additional problem if one is trying to avoid gendered references to God. One of Psalm 23's wonderful qualities is that it starts off with God being distant from the poet, a message underscored by all references to God in the third person, "He." In the second half of the Psalm, God is felt more directly and is referred to solely in the more personal second person, "You." This literary device works well in the Hebrew but to replace the impersonal "He" with "God" would undermine this embedded literary gem. So here, too, I made an exception.

I ask the reader's understanding that often, but not always, we can bridge the gap between a faithful translation and a commitment to non-gendered language.

How to Find a Biblical Verse

It is common to denote Bible verses with two numbers, separated by a colon. The first number is the chapter—or in the case of this book, the Psalm. The second number is the verse. For example, Psalm 23 and verse 2 would be written 23:2. If we are citing multiple verses, for example Psalm 23 verses 2 through 5, it would be written 23:2-5.

And now, welcome to the wonderful world of the Psalms. *May God grant your heart's desire and fulfill your every plan* (Psalms 20:5), and may the words of the Psalms speak to and for your heart.

—RABBI ALLAN BERKOWITZ

The
Psalms

Psalm 1

1 Happy is the person that does not walk in the counsel of the wicked, nor stands in the way of sinners, nor sits in the seat of the scorners.

2 But his delight is in the teaching of God; and he studies that teaching day and night.

3 And he is like a tree planted by the rivers of water, that brings forth fruit in season; whose foliage never withers; and whatever it produces, thrives.

4 Not so the wicked; they are like the chaff which the wind drives away.

5 Therefore the wicked shall not survive judgment, nor will sinners, in the congregation of the righteous.

6 For God knows the way of the righteous: but the way of the wicked is doomed.

"Happinesses"

Imagine David the lonesome shepherd wandering the hills above Jerusalem as he reflects on life. Amidst the solitude and silence (except for the occasional bleating of his sheep, of course), he considers the uplifts and tragedies of the human condition. His sensitive soul is moved to write poetry representing two perspectives. He writes as a shepherd reflecting on his flock, and he writes about God, the eternal Shepherd, tending to the human flock.

This first Psalm is both an introduction to David's philosophy of life and a fitting introduction to the whole collection. In six short verses, the poet is saying, "Nothing will stir your soul quite like this journey through the Psalms that I've prepared for you."

Psalm 1 is the thesis statement that guides David's philosophy of life. He says:

> *Happy is the person who has not followed the counsel of the wicked, or taken the path of sinners, or joined the company of the insolent; rather, the teaching of God is a delight, study it day and night.*

We need to be mindful that David was a religious man, a man of God. So, naturally, his worldview is centered around the teachings of the Eternal Shepherd. Here in Psalm 1, he offers us a life lesson and a bit of a paradox. The life lesson is about traveling the road to contentment. In David's world view, there are righteous actions and sinful actions, and happiness and contentment are earned in relationship to our pursuit of wholesome living.

And the paradox? David warns that happiness is connected to carefully assessing from whom we should and should not seek advice. Take note that to achieve this happiness we must accept his advice about accepting advice. It's a good thing that David, who at times was a deeply flawed human being, crafted a collection of Psalms filled with wisdom worthy of our attention.

If You're Happy and You Know It, Read This Psalm

Jewish commentators have noted that the Hebrew word for "happy" in verse one is *ashrei*, and it comes with a twist. The word is actually in the plural form, "happinesses." There are eight Psalms[1] that use this word and each time it is pluralized. The Psalmist is teaching us that happiness is not a singular condition, but rather a collection of positive experiences and states of mind assembled over a period of time. This Psalm asks us to consider the many times and many ways we experience happiness and contentment in our own lives.

SOUL STEPS

ACHIEVING IMMORTALITY THROUGH OUR ACTIONS

We read in Verse 3:

> And he is like a tree planted by the rivers of water, that brings forth fruit in season; whose foliage never withers; and whatever it produces, thrives.

[1] Psalms 1, 2, 32, 33, 34, 40, 41, 65

Comparing a righteous person to a tree *whose foliage never withers* is taken to mean that through our good deeds do we attain immortality. David's philosophy of life can be summed up this way: There is good and there is evil; a life of reward comes with the former and punishment with the latter; and eternal life is the reward for righteous living. Find a quiet space, preferably an inspiring place, and reflect on what in your life you would like to see become an eternal reminder of the good you do in the world.

AN ABUNDANCE OF HAPPINESS

As we learned above, the Psalms always use the plural form of the word *ashrei*, best translated into a word that doesn't exist in English—"happinesses." This suggests a multitude of happiness and acknowledges different states of happiness. With this perspective in mind, reflect on the positive experiences and realities of your life. Can you discern degrees of contentment and joy? What brings you extreme happiness? What are the pleasures in your life worthy of gratitude? Consider starting a gratitude journal to help you discern and reflect on the many different "happinesses" in your life.

WHO WROTE THE BOOK OF PSALMS?

In the introduction to this book, we noted that Jewish tradition considers David to have written the Psalms, while Biblical scholars suggest only some, but certainly not all, of the Psalms were written by him. Let's understand a little more about the authorship question.

David is credited with introducing music as a form of worship. And since many of the Psalms are musical compositions involving choirs and orchestras, it seems that David became closely associated with the Psalms because of this musical connection. Scholars, however, suggest that many of the Psalms traditionally credited to David are actually later compositions composed to honor David. They offer dedications such as "A Song of David," "For David," "To David."

And so, in this book, we use "David" to refer to the generic author in order to render the texts and the commentaries readable and accessible. In doing so, it suggests that whether it was David or a later poet, in both cases we inherited texts that hold the reflections of a deeply sensitive soul, an expert observer of the human condition, and a writer who was so very skillful in communicating both about life and our emotions.

Psalm 7

1 Shiggayon of David, which he sang to God, concerning Cush the Benjaminite.

2 O God, my God, in You I seek refuge; deliver me from all my pursuers and save me,

3 lest, he tears me apart like a lion, rending in pieces, and no one to save me.

4 O God, my God, if I have done such things, if my hands bear the guilt of wrongdoing,

5 If I have dealt evil to my ally—I who rescued my foe without reward—

6 Then let the enemy pursue and overtake me; let him trample my life to the ground, and lay my body in the dust. Selah.

7 Rise, O God, in Your anger; assert Yourself against the fury of my foes;
Awake for me; You have commanded judgment.

8 Let the assembly of peoples gather about You, with You enthroned above, on high.

9 God judges the peoples; Judge me, O God, according to the righteousness and blamelessness that are mine.

10 Let the evil of the wicked come to an end, but establish the righteous; the righteous God probes the mind and conscience.

11 I look to God to shield me; the deliverer of the upright.

12 God vindicates the righteous; God pronounces indignation each day.

13 If one does not turn back, but whets his sword, bends his bow and aims it,

14   *Then against himself he readies deadly weapons, and makes his arrows sharp.*

15   *Behold, he hatches evil, conceives mischief, and gives birth to fraud.*

16   *He has dug a pit and deepened it, and will fall into the trap he made.*

17   *His mischief will fall upon his own head; his violence will come down upon his skull.*

18   *I will praise God for God's righteousness, and sing a hymn to the name of the God Most High.*

Growing Beyond Hate

Psalm 7 is the equal of the finest Hollywood drama. Pursued by enemies, David is distressed, frightened, and over-whelmed. From the depths of despair his soul cries out to God. So human and so relatable—who hasn't experienced moments of dread without praying for relief? The Psalmist takes us on a literary journey of fear, panic, and loss of hope, and on a return to faith and the belief that God will protect. And when the threat has passed, his soul exhales a song of jubilation.

The first verse of our Psalm is a headline identifying David as the author and God as the audience, and it references Cush the Benjaminite. This may allude to King Saul and the dra-matic events recorded in the First Book of Samuel (chapter 24). Saul sought to destroy David, who took refuge in a desert cave at Ein Gedi, near the Dead Sea. Fatigued from the pur-suit, King Saul coincidentally enters that same cave to rest, unaware that David is there too. As David contemplates this juicy plot twist, he goes through a cycle of emotions and a journey of personal growth: joy that God delivered his enemy into his hands; regret that his relationship with the king has devolved to this; and remorse for wanting to harm Saul. In the end, David acknowledges it is for God alone to judge Saul.

Tradition tells us this Psalm was written when David chose not to harm Saul. It is a poem celebrating David's per-sonal spiritual growth and his ability to overcome the basest of human emotions: the thirst for revenge. In the end, this remarkable Psalm uses a dramatic piece of history to teach us that our fears do not justify inflicting harm on others.

The Enigma of Shiggayon

The Psalmist opens this piece by declaring it is a "Shiggayon of David." Our problem is that we don't know what a "Shiggayon" is. One theory is that it is a kind of ancient musical instrument. Another suggests that the word means *error* and reflects a poem that speaks of David's remorse for seeking Saul's downfall. And a third suggestion, by the biblical scholar Robert Alter, is that this musical piece is a rhapsody—that is, an artistic offering that is filled with ecstatic emotion.

Pun and Punishment

Jewish tradition connects this Psalm to the holiday of *Purim* based on two linguistic references in both this Psalm and the *Megillah* (the Book of Esther read on Purim). The Psalm mentions "Cush the Benjaminite," and the Book of Esther refers to "Mordechai the Benjaminite." So it turns out that Mordechai is a descendent of King Saul! A second linguistic connection involves the word *tzorer*, or *pursuer*. The same word appears in both the Psalm (in verses 5 and 7) and the *Megillah* (in 9:10, *Haman, the pursuer of the Jews*). And take note that both narratives are about a Jewish leader pursued by an enemy seeking their destruction.

SOUL STEPS

MANAGING OUR ANGER

To be human is to get angry, and how we channel that anger is a great challenge. Not allowing ourselves to get angry bottles up a very real emotion and inflicts harm on ourselves. Venting that anger without control is a very real problem, as well. Finding the right balance has confounded even the greatest peacemakers. Would it surprise you to know that even Martin Luther King Jr. and Gandhi admitted that anger was a personal challenge to be conquered? With this awareness in mind, conduct an "anger audit" on yourself. Think about the times you get angry. Are you generally comfortable with how you respond to them? Some questions to ask yourself:

> *What kinds of things make me angry?*
> *Do I properly react or overreact to them?*
> *How could I communicate my intense feelings in*
> *a way that might yield more productive results?*

It might take time to reprogram yourself to respond more productively to anger. If at times you don't (yet!) react differently and your anger arises once again, remind yourself that you are on a journey. It may take time to change. And when you do successfully change your response to anger, think of Psalm 7. Like David, you should celebrate for having avoided a negative response.

PASTORAL POEMS OR ODES TO VIOLENCE?

The Psalms suffer from a confused identity. On the one hand, they are thought of as the pastoral reflections of a soulful shepherd; on the other, many Psalms express anger, reference violence, and pray for harsh Divine retribution. So, which is it? Are they idealistic poetry or celebrations of brutality?

The answer is both. Within the collection of 150 Psalms we find many that are militaristic and violent. Others, like Psalm 23, "The Lord is My Shepherd," are pastoral and reflect on the fragile human condition. And while some readers may recoil at the violence, it does reflect the Biblical reality. The ancient world (the modern world, too) was often violent and bloody. Biblical authors rarely shied away from reflecting their reality.

So how should we understand the dualism of pastoral poetry and violent epochs?

Perhaps they reflect the tension we feel when we consider ourselves to be good people on the one hand, and yet we sometimes experience anger, rage, and thoughts of revenge.

Psalm 15

1 A Psalm of David. God, who may abide in Your tent, who may dwell on Your holy mountain?

2 One who walks without blame, who does what is just, and whose heart speaks the truth;

3 Whose tongue is not given to evil; who does not harm other, nor brings reproach to a neighbor;

4 In whose eyes an abhorrent person is despised, and who honors those who hold God in awe; who stands by an oath even to one's detriment;

5 Who never lends money with interest, or accepts a bribe against the innocent. The one who acts thusly shall never stumble.

Taking Stock of One's Soul

In five short verses, Psalm 15 offers a philosophy of life for the ancient observant Jew—and maybe for us, too! The Psalm opens with a bold question:

> God, who may abide in Your tent, who may dwell
> on Your holy mountain?

The Psalm then answers this question in the remaining four verses.

Verse 2: One who walks without blame, who does what is just, and whose heart speaks the truth;

Verse 3: Whose tongue is not given to evil; who does not harm other, nor brings reproach to a neighbor;

Verse 4: In whose eyes an abhorrent person is despised, and who honors those who hold God in awe; who stands by an oath even to one's detriment;

Verse 5: Who never lends money with interest, or accepts a bribe against the innocent. The one who acts thusly shall never stumble.

All of the Torah's commandments can be placed in two categories: the commandments that regulate our behavior toward human beings and the commandments that regulate our behavior before God. We see this idea in Psalm 15 which tells us we cannot be right with God if we are not right in our behavior toward other human beings.

Another way of categorizing the 613 commandments is to divide them into positive and negative decrees—in other words, in one group are the actions we should take and in the other are the actions we should not. We see this in Psalm 15, too, where we are told to *act justly* and *speak truth*—both positive commands—and also *do not speak evil, do not harm others*, in the negative column.

You'll notice that in each of the lines where the Psalm provides answers to the question, the answers come in batches of three per line. There are three references to how we act toward other people and three referring to how we behave before God; there are three positive commandments and three negatives.

Furthermore, the Talmud—the great repository of law and lore compiled between 200–500 CE—suggests that in this Psalm, David distilled the commandments into a smaller list of the most essential, namely those represented by the threefold answers to the Psalm's question in verses 2–5.

For such a compact poem, it packs quite a punch! It is a philosophy of life: a suggestion that we remain mindful of both God and humankind in our lives. There is even a summary of the commandments in the Torah! As belief systems go, one could do no better than living by the values expressed in Psalm 15.

Elevating the Mind before Ascending the Mountain

When the Israelites would make pilgrimage to ancient Jerusalem, it was customary for them to spend the night on the city's doorstep before ascending to the Temple Mount to present their offerings. During this time, they were expected to reflect on the purity of their souls. Some believe that Psalm 15 was the basis for this reflection: We can imagine the pilgrim asking the communal leader, perhaps a priest, a sage, or a teacher, the Psalm's question, "*Who may abide in Your tent, who may dwell on Your holy mountain?*", and that the answer to these questions came in the form of Psalm 15. Or, it may have been the pilgrims themselves who reflected on the question and studied the Psalm's answer.

Either way, this custom suggests that the pilgrim was to spend the night reflecting on the proper values with which to live one's life—certainly a worthy exercise to foster the proper frame of mind before ascending to God's mountain.

SOUL STEPS

KNOWING OUR VALUES

Have you ever considered what you stand for? Make a list of the eight or ten most important values you hold. Which of the Psalmist's values in verses 2–5 would also be on your list? What, in your opinion, did the Psalmist leave out? Are there values on the Psalmist's list or your list that you think should be universally held by all? Consider what the world would be like if everyone held your values? If you have children or young adults in your life, ask them to reflect on the values they think are most important. It might be interesting to discuss how your values and theirs are similar and different.

Psalm 23

1   A Psalm of David.
The Lord is my shepherd; I shall not want.

2   He has me lie down in green pastures;
He leads me beside the still waters.

3   He restores my soul;
He guides me in straight paths for His name's sake.

4   Though I walk through the valley of the shadow of death,
I fear no harm, for You are with me;
Your rod and Your staff comfort me.

5   You prepare a table before me in the presence of my enemies;
You anointed my head with oil; my cup overflows.

6   Surely goodness and mercy will follow me all the days of my life;
And I will dwell in the house of God forever.

Finding God in the Shadows

Is there a Psalm with greater brand recognition than Psalm 23? Its opening verse, *The Lord is my shepherd, I shall not want,* is universally familiar. Psalm 23 evokes pathos, thus it is recited at funerals and is borne deeply in many hearts as a comforting mantra for God's personal protection. It is a poetic blanket that wraps us in warmth and comfort.

We can easily imagine the poetic synapses firing in David's head as he realizes that the very nurturing, guiding, and protecting that he offers his flock parallel the actions of God the Shepherd nurturing the human flock. And indeed Psalm 23 kindles its messages by relying on the metaphor of the shepherd, using the language and tools of the sheep-herding trade. Deeply, marvelously, craftily, this Psalm nurtures and protects our souls with the care of a loving shepherd whose job it is to steer the flock safely through the journey.

What is the impact of the many shepherding metaphors? Just as a shepherd guides the flock to pastures for sustenance, God guides us and provides for us. Literally and figuratively, the flock feels protected, adequately provisioned, and pastorally comforted.

The poetic words run deep. Consider verse 4. The first half of the verse is the well-known phrase that is often translated as *Though I walk in the valley of death.* But a more exact translation is *Though I walk through the valley of the shadow of death,* a descriptive reflection of the way the shepherd guides the flock through a canyon as the topography shields them from the sun. The sudden darkness, similar to the kind we experience in life's bleaker moments, can be scary.

But then, the second half of verse 4 tells us, *I fear no harm for You are with me; Your staff and your rod do comfort me.* The Hebrew words *shivtekha* and *mishantekha*—staff and rod—are tools of the shepherd's trade. The shepherd's staff is used to gently redirect an errant lamb, and the rod is his walking stick that keeps him on the right path. So, through David's poetry, we realize that the Shepherd, like the shepherd, is right there to guide us through the canyons of life that may frighten us.

Psalm 23 has a powerful embedded secret that plays on our emotions. The way the writer of the poem refers to God changes mid-poem, from the third person (*He leads me*) to the second person (*You are with me*). And when is the exact moment that this switch from a distant God to a personal and protecting God happens? In verse 4:

> *Though I walk through the valley of the shadow of death,*
> > *I fear no harm, for You are with me;*

At the very moment, when fear is at its worst—when the sheep and we are feeling the most vulnerable—You, God, are with me. When we walk through the valley of death, that is when we need the Shepherd to be closest and most nurturing.

Neither David the poet nor God disappoints.

A Little God Goes a Long Way

For a Psalm that so deeply conveys the loving protection of the Divine, it is fascinating that God's name is only mentioned twice, in the first and last verses. The Psalmist seems to be noting (for himself and us) that sometimes we feel God's profound presence in subtle and quiet ways.

A *Verdant* Verse
Verse 5 reads, *You anointed my head with oil.* There was an early Near Eastern custom to pour oil over the head as a symbol of abundance and contentment. We can imagine the peace and solitude of both the shepherd and the sheep as they reposed in green meadows, a gentle breeze blowing, and seemingly not a care in the world. The pastoral calm soothed the soul, quieted any anxiety, and was a moment when David felt particularly safe and content in his life.

SOUL STEPS

AN ANCIENT PRACTICE, A NEW OPPORTUNITY
The Jewish custom of placing a rock on the headstone when we visit a grave hearkens back to a shepherding practice in the ancient world. A shepherd (David included, no doubt) would carry a leather satchel containing one pebble for each sheep in the herd. Periodically, the shepherd would count the animals by removing a pebble as each sheep passed him. In this way, he could know if any sheep went astray. Today, we place a pebble on a headstone as if to say, "We are keeping track of this beloved soul who passed before us. This one counts."

The next time you visit the gravesite of a loved one or friend, read Psalm 23 and ask yourself, How does this beloved soul still count? How does this person's legacy still endure?

SHEPHERDING A BETTER PERSPECTIVE ON SHABBAT
Psalm 23 speaks of God's providence in our lives, so some Jews recite it on Shabbat—a day to reflect on the joys and

abundance in our lives. Bring this Psalm to your Friday dinner table and reflect on the bounties and the challenges you experienced in the past week. How did you feel nurtured by life this week? Were there moments when you felt alone or distant from the "flock of humanity"?

PASSOVER MANNA

There is a custom to recite Psalm 23 at the Passover *Seder*. This is based on the Talmud's suggestion that the verse *The Lord is my shepherd, I shall not want* is a reference to the manna provided to the Israelites in the desert. Enrich your *Seder* by reading Psalm 23 and asking your guests, "What is the manna that life blessed you with since last Passover?"

THE PSALMS IN JEWISH LIFE

There are few things that animate Jewish life more than reciting Psalms. Psalms are integrated into the morning, afternoon, and evening prayer services each day. There is a designated Psalm for each day of the week, one for the occurrence of each new month, a special Psalm for Chanukah, as well as before, during, and after the High Holy Days.

Traditionally, Jews turn to Psalms when words might fail us. They can be recited by a patient in need of healing and they can be recited on the patient's behalf by well-wishers, and they play a prominent role in Jewish mourning rituals. "Soul guardians" sit with the casket before burial and recite Psalms beseeching God to protect this soul. The funeral service includes Psalms, as does the prayer service in the mourner's home during the week of Shiva. When visiting a gravesite, we recite them as well.

Historically, Jewish communities gather in times of calamity to recite Psalms, often accompanied by fasting. Similarly, individual Jews turn to Psalms when facing personal crises. Why have the Psalms taken this prominent place in Jewish life? The answer centers on the state of mind of the reciter: overwhelmed, confused, emotionally lost, filled with gratitude, introspective, despairing, hyper-attentive to the moment, relieved, speechless, physically or emotionally pained.

The Psalms are also special in the way they address the peak experiences we encounter in life, something we don't see in other Biblical texts. There is very good alignment between the Psalms' focus on these human experiences and our need to process our emotions when we encounter similar life experiences. It makes sense that the Psalms, so reflective of the human condition, are featured prominently in Jewish life.

Psalm 30

1 A Psalm song for the dedication of the House. Of David.

2 I extol You, O God for You have lifted me up, and did not let my enemies rejoice over me.

3 O God, my God, I cried out to You, and You healed me.

4 O God, You brought me up from Sheol, sustained me in life that I should not go down into the Pit.

5 Sing to God, you pious ones, praise God's holiness.

6 For God is angry but a moment, and when pleased, there is life.
One may lie down weeping at night; but at dawn there is joy. `

7 When I was untroubled, I thought, "I shall never be shaken,"

8 for You, O God, when You were pleased, You made me firm as a mighty mountain. When You hid Your face, I was terrified.

9 I called to You, O God; to my God I made appeal,

10 "What is to be gained from my death, from my descent into the Pit? Can dust praise You? Can it declare Your truth?

11 Hear, O God and have mercy on me; O God, be my help!"

12 You turned my mourning into dancing, you undid my sack-cloth and offered me joy,

13 that my being might sing hymns to You unceasingly; O God, my God, I will thank You forever.

Dedication: To House, God, and Life

This seemingly straightforward Psalm is brimming with challenges. The first challenge is found in two competing themes pursued by the Psalm, so it confuses us to know what this Psalm is saying. One theme is a personal prayer of salvation written by one who was ill–perhaps deathly ill. With renewal and the relief that comes with a return to life, the appreciative soul was moved to write a personal prayer of thanksgiving.

Within the Psalm, several phrases support this thematic understanding: You lifted me up; You healed me; Sustained my life; What is to be gained from my death?; You turned my mourning into dancing. And within this, there is a sub-theme we notice: through the fog of illness the writer fears that their enemies will rejoice if they succumb to illness.

And the second theme? Because the opening verse speaks of *dedicating the House*, some see this Psalm as a piece written as an ode to a sacred abode. This school of thought offers three possibilities:

1. It was written to celebrate Solomon's Temple in Jerusalem,
2. It was written by David at the dedication of an earlier and more localized altar for God,
3. It was written for the dedication of someone's personal home.

So, our first challenge is to figure out the Psalm's purpose and message.

The second challenge we face is one of literary continuity within the text, for the text contradicts itself no matter which of the two themes we select. If Psalm 30 is a personal prayer of thanksgiving, then how do we make sense of the first verse? In a piece that speaks of grave illness, pleads with God for healing, and expresses joy upon recovery, what then is meant by dedicating this piece to the House of God? Some scholars help us around this challenge by suggesting that the first verse was not part of the original poem, instead it was appended at a later time by a different author.

And if the Psalm is written to celebrate the dedication of a sacred space (a temple, the Temple, or a private home), how are we to understand the illness theme? This seemingly simple piece is, in fact, quite enigmatic.

Rhythm and Rhyme

The Hebrew in this Psalm offers intriguing word plays. It employs rhyming words and we suspect this is intentional. One interesting example is verse 12, in which four of the eight Hebrew words rhyme. The effect of rhyming words is to create a sense of movement, in this case movement that parallels the content. Through rhyming words, the Psalm contrasts *mourning* with *dancing* and *sackcloth* (the garment worn by a mourner) with *joy*.

In the ancient world, the act of mourning had a physical manifestation, a rhythmic swaying. Our Psalm digs deep and contrasts the mournful swaying with a dance of joy. So the rhyming structure of the Psalm adds movement to the words of the Psalm, words that speak of movement. You might say that the rhythm and rhyme of the Psalm create literary harmony.

SOUL STEPS

MILESTONES

Psalm 30 reflects on many life situations we experience: the dedication of a house, a recovery from illness, a series of frightful moments, and the emotional lift that follows dark times. Review the Psalm and identify the milestones it references. For example, the opening verse references a dedication of the house. You might reflect on your feelings upon moving into a new residence: "God, I am excited to inaugurate this new home. May it be a place of joy and blessings for my family."

For each moment you identify, consider how you might feel in that situation. You might even prepare a written reflection that links your state of mind to the life event.

Consider reciting Psalm 30 when younger family members experience a momentous transition: when a young child is moving into his/her own room, or transitioning from a crib to a bed.

WHO WAS DAVID?

Musician, shepherd, warrior, king, ruthless politician, deeply flawed parent, and one of the greatest Jewish leaders ever. David was multi-faceted and complex, bloodthirsty and soulful, a man of war and a man of words, poetry and song.

David's rise to prominence began when he gained King Saul's favor after a series of military victories, including the battle of David vs. Goliath. Years later, he was forced into exile when Saul jealously feared David's popularity with the people.

David was extremely charismatic. His passion and compassion garnered him a small army of equally troubled souls.

David was so politically astute that he managed to become King even though one of Saul's heirs was in line for the throne. And David could be ruthless: He was smitten with Batsheva, a woman married to a soldier named Uriah, so he arranged for Uriah to be sent to the front lines where he would be killed in battle, setting Batsheva free to marry David.

He was the flawed father who endured multiple attempted coups by his own sons. And he was the Jewish leader who elevated Jerusalem as the ritual center of the nation. He brought the Ark of the Covenant up to Jerusalem, built an altar, and planned for the building of the Great Temple. To this very day the City of David stands prominently in Jerusalem.

According to Jewish tradition, he was physically strong and quite attractive. He was a poet, a masterful musician, and being the enigma that he was, he was forbidden by God to build the Temple because he was a warrior with blood on his hands.

So, who was David? He was a person of many contradictions and inconsistencies; a man filled with passion, talents, and flaws. In other words, he was deeply human and through the Psalms we too can appreciate our contradictions—our passions, our talents, our flaws that add up to our own humanity.

Psalm 55

¹ For the Conductor; with instrumental music. A maskil of David.

² Hear my prayer, O God; do not ignore my plea.

³ Pay heed to me, and answer me; I am tossed about, complaining and moaning;

⁴ Because of the voice of the enemy, because of the oppression of the wicked;
For they bring evil upon me, and furiously harass me.

⁵ My heart is convulsed within me; terrors of death assail me.

⁶ Fear and trembling invade me, I am clothed in horror.

⁷ I said: "Oh that I had wings like a dove! I would fly away and find rest.

⁸ Surely, I would flee far off, I would lodge in the wilderness. Selah

⁹ I would soon find me a shelter from the stormy wind and tempest."

¹⁰ O God, confound their speech; for I see lawlessness and strife in the city.

¹¹ Day and night they make their rounds on the walls; evil and mischief are inside.

¹² Malice is within it; fraud and deceit never leave its square.

¹³ It is not an enemy who reviles me; I could bear that.
It is not my foe who vaunts himself against me; I could hide from him.

¹⁴ But it is you, my equal, my companion, my friend;

¹⁵ *Sweet was our fellowship; we walked together in God's house.*

¹⁶ May God incite death against them, let them go down alive into the netherworld;
For where they dwell, there evil is.

¹⁷ As for me, I call to God; and God will deliver me.

¹⁸ Evening, morning, and noon, I complain, and moan; and God hears my voice.

¹⁹ God redeems my soul unharmed from the battle against me; it is as though many are on my side.

²⁰ God who has reigned from the first, who will have no successor, hears and humbles those who have no fear of God.

²¹ He harmed his ally, he broke his pact;

²² His talk was smoother than butter, yet his mind was on war; his words were more soothing than oil, yet they were drawn swords.

²³ Cast your burden upon God, Who will sustain you;
God will never let the righteous person collapse.

²⁴ For You, O God, will bring them down into the nethermost pit;
Those murderous, treacherous men shall not live out half their days;
But as for me, I will trust in You.

When a Friend Betrays Us

What would cause David to write these words of dread?

> I am tossed about moaning. My heart is convulsed within me.
> Fear and trembling invade me. I am clothed in horror.

If you have ever been betrayed by a friend, then you will relate to the searing pain of the heart that is Psalm 55. King David faces a palace coup orchestrated by his own son, Absalom. As the rebellion unfolds and its ultimate success or failure hangs in the balance, David worries about the impacts on the nation, for he knows that revolutions often impose terrible burdens on people. He cries out to God, I see lawlessness and strife in the city.

As bad as it must have been to face a challenge to his authority by his own son and simultaneously to worry about civil unrest, that is not the source of his deepest pain. David discovers that his close friend and confidant, Achitophel, was secretly advising Absalom. Psalm 55 offers these beautiful, tragic, mournful words that lay bare David's soul:

> It is not an enemy who reviles me; I could bear that.
> It is not my foe who vaunts himself against me; I could hide from him.
> But it is you my equal, my companion, my friend.

Sweet was our fellowship; we walked together
in God's house.

There is a literary progression in this Psalm that shows the emotional undulations we experience when suffering heavy burdens or fears. The Psalm—and often our own psyches—begins with a very heartfelt prayer to God, *Hear my prayer, do not ignore my plea.* It is so very common, so very human, to plead with God at the moment we are overwhelmed and feeling threatened.

It is also a very human reaction to want to escape the tyranny of the moment. In David's words:

Oh that I had the wings of a dove! I would fly
away and find rest . . .
I would lodge in the wilderness.
I would soon find me a shelter from the stormy
wind and tempest.

What prevents him from fleeing is his sense of obligation. David overcomes the urge to run away for he needs to be with his community in times of trouble. This reflects a timeless human need for we, too, overcome our urge to flee so we can be with our support community in times of trouble.

Next, David begins to confront the betrayal at the hands of his once-close friend. His emotions swing back and forth between his personal pain and a sense of obligation to those around him. The Psalm closes with David arriving at a stage of acceptance and with a path forward: David will place his faith, his prayers, and his trust in God. He may not know how or when, but he believes that good will vanquish the evil he has experienced and his life will be sustained.

This is a beautifully written and sensitive Psalm. It speaks through deep emotional pain and reveals the personal scars of one who has suffered betrayal at the hands of a trusted soulmate.

Pain and Wisdom

The introductory verse to our Psalm reads, *For the conductor, with instrumental music, a Maskil of David.* What is a *maskil*? Our tradition is unsure. The word might best be translated as *a lesson acquired through wisdom,* and there are two common theories about its use in the fourteen Psalms where it is found. The first is that these musical compositions were for specially trained Levites who acquired the musical wisdom to perform them. The second explanation is that the Psalm itself offers a lesson based on wisdom David learned through his life—a morality play of sorts. No doubt the betrayal and pain he suffered taught him valuable lessons. Like David, we cannot escape pain and suffering in our lives. However, we too can write a new song to guide the way forward, a song composed of notes acquired through wisdom.

SOUL STEPS

OVERCOMING OUR NIGHTMARES

In the Talmud, we find an unusual ancient ritual for processing nightmares[1]. The ritual includes verse 19 of our Psalm: *God redeems my soul unharmed from the battle against me; it is as though many are on my side.* If one is troubled by a dream (in the Psalms' words, *the battle against me*), it should be shared with three friends (*many are on my side*). The friends recite a series of Biblical verses that focus on the concepts of turning (*May God turn this dream from bad to good*), redeeming (*May*

[1] Talmud Berakhot 55b

God redeem this soul from the burden), and peace *(May this soul be calmed)*.

Reflect on verse 19. Take note that the poet, in the first half of the verse, credits God for redeeming his burdened soul, while in the second half of the verse he says the redemption came through the presence of friends standing with him. In other words, the poet's friends were God's instrument of redemption, and because of them, his nightmare was abated.

When you reflect on the tough times in your life, who were God's messengers that helped turn your situation around, redeemed your soul, and restored a measure of peace to you?

FIRST VERSES

Who? When? How? One hundred and sixteen Psalms offer a first verse with an informational clue that tells us something about the intention of the Psalm. Generally, the opening verse either reminds us of the identity of the author ("A Song of David"), dedicates the poem to someone ("For Moses"), instructs the Temple musicians how to play the piece (fifty-five Psalms start with "To the Conductor"), references where or when the Psalm was first used (such as a pilgrimage to Jerusalem), or defines what kind of poem it is (a song, a prayer, a supplication). In total, there are more than sixty kinds of instructions in the opening lines of the Psalms. So, when we read one, we should take note of its first verse. It has a lot to say.

Psalm 67

1 For the Conductor; with instrumental music. A Psalm, a song.

2 May God be gracious to us, and bless us;
May God show us favor; Selah

3 That your way may be known on earth, Your salvation among all nations.

4 Let the peoples give thanks to You, O God;
Let the peoples give thanks unto You, all of them.

5 Nations exult and shout for joy;
For You will judge the peoples with equity,
And lead the nations upon earth.   Selah

6 Let the peoples give thanks to You, O God;
Let the peoples give thanks to You, all of them.

7 May the earth yield its produce; May God, our God, bless us.

8 May God bless us; and be revered to the ends of the earth.

A Menorah of Gratitude

A delightful poem in a mere eight verses, and it bears a secret, too! Before we explore its hidden treat, let's understand that Psalm 67 sings praises to God for blessings bestowed on Israel, for publicizing Israel's salvation to the world, and for inspiring other nations to thank God. It would appear that this was a musical piece performed in the Great Temple.

As we have seen with other Psalms, often the Psalmist embedded musical instructions for the conductor, the choir, and the musicians who performed the piece at the Great Temple. Psalm 67 is believed to have been composed for two choirs and the congregation to chant responsively. Its opening verse reads, *For the Conductor with instrumental music, a Psalm, a song.* And twice within the text, we find the word *selah*—a musical notation for the choir or musical director.

Given the themes of this poem—God's blessings, the publicizing of salvation, and hope that other nations will be inspired to thank God—it seems appropriate that this would be crafted as a musical composition. Music is itself a vehicle that amplifies, broadcasts, and inspires.

Now, about that secret. The secret in Psalm 67 is revealed through the poem's internal symmetry where a close reading reveals perfect inner parallelism. Consider:

- Verse 1 offers musical instructions to the choir, while verses 2–8 constitute the Psalm itself.
- The first verse of the actual Psalm (verse 2) and the last verse (verse 8) both ask for God's blessings.

- Verses 3 and 7 also parallel each other, as they speak of the earth.
- Verses 4 and 6 both express the hope that all people will acknowledge God.
- The uncoupled middle verse, verse 5, serves as the musical fulcrum. At the center of this Psalm with its themes of blessings and salvation is verse 5 which says, for all these blessings, joyously sing to God.

This internal symmetry yields an artistic delight as these verses can be visually crafted as a *menorah*. Since the first and last verses offer parallel content, as do the second and second to last verses, and the two middle verses, by drawing a line between a verse and its thematic companion, what results is a *menorah* (see illustration).

Throughout Jewish history, synagogues and pious Jews in their homes have fashioned a wall hanging called a *shviti*. *Shviti* means I *will place* and is part of the traditional expression, I *will place God before me always* (found in Psalm 16:8). Because Psalm 67's internal symmetry is so beautifully represented as a *menorah*, it is often used for the creation of a *shviti*, with each *menorah* branch created from the words of the verses.

Priestly Blessings

Though music in the Great Temple was the domain of the Levites, this Psalm pays homage to the Kohanim, too. A careful reading will reveal that verse 2 hints at the Priestly Blessing found in the Torah:[1]

> *God be gracious to us, bless us, and may God's face shine upon us.*

Feeling God's Presence

Similar to Psalm 23, "The Lord Is My Shepherd," this Psalm alternates between referring to God in the impersonal third person ("He") and the more intimate second person ("You"). It may be that this switching, combined with the call and response between the congregation and the choirs, created a sense of change regarding God's presence in our lives. For David—and for us—there are times we sense God's closeness and there are times we long for it.

Fun with Numbers

This Psalm plays with the number 49. Aside from the musical instructions, there are forty-nine words, and the middle verse, verse 5, has forty-nine letters. Why is the number forty-nine meaningful? The Jewish mystics connected this Psalm with the forty-nine days between Passover and Shavuot when we celebrate the spring wheat harvest. And as if to seal the deal, verse 7 even says, *May the earth yield its produce: May God, our God, bless us.*

---

[1] Numbers 6:24-26

SOUL STEPS

CRAFTING A *MENORAH* OF GRATITUDE

The Psalms can help guide children, too. Share Psalm 67 with children, explaining that this poem speaks about the blessings that life gives us. After showing them how the verses can be written to create a *menorah*, ask them to identify seven things for which they are thankful. A fun craft exercise is to turn their seven reflections into a personal menorah of gratitude.

REFLECTING ON THE LIGHT IN OUR LIVES

Some Sephardic and Chasidic Jews recite this Psalm nightly to remember the Great Temple. And we learned that many Jews use this Psalm artistically to keep God ever present. Try this spiritual exercise: Late at night, recite Psalm 67 and ponder, *What do I always want to remember, and what will keep me mindful of it in the future?*

THE MANY WAYS TO PRAISE

The great 11th century Biblical commentator Rashi identified ten different forms of musical praise in the Book of Psalms. They are:

Nitzuakh – orchestral composition

Niggun – soulful melody

Mizmor – musical poetry

Shir –song

Hallel – poem of praise

Tefilla – prayer

Berakha –blessing

Hoda'ah – thanksgiving

Ashrei – expressions of happiness

Halleluyah – praise to God.

Rashi further connected this to the first two words of the entire Book of Psalms – *Ashrei ha-ish* ('*Happy is the one who...*'). The contentment we experience in life should be expressed through song, soulful melody, expressions of thanksgiving, praise to God, recognitions of blessings, and more.

For the author of the Psalms, righteous living results in happiness. For Rashi, happiness results in multiple expressions of our joy.

Psalm 72

1 Of Solomon.

O God, endow the king with Your judgments, the king's son with Your righteousness;

2 that he may judge Your people rightly, Your lowly ones, justly.

3 Let the mountains produce well-being for the people, the hills, the reward of justice.

4 Let him champion the lowly among the people, deliver the needy folk, and crush those who wrong them.

5 Let them fear You as long as the sun shines, while the moon lasts, generations on end.

6 Let him be like rain that falls on a mown field, like a downpour of rain on the ground,

7 that the righteous may flourish in his time, and well-being abound, till the moon is no more.

8 Let him rule from sea to sea, from the river to the ends of the earth.

9 Let desert-dwellers kneel before him, and his enemies lick the dust.

10 Let kings of Tarshish and the islands pay tribute, kings of Sheba and Seba offer gifts.

11 Let all kings bow to him, and all nations serve him.

12 For he saves the needy who cry out, the lowly who have no helper.

13 He cares about the poor and the needy; He brings the needy deliverance.

14   *He redeems them from fraud and lawlessness; the shedding of their blood weighs heavily upon him.*

15   *So let him live, and receive gold of Sheba; let prayers for him be said always, blessings on him invoked at all times.*

16   *Let abundant grain be in the land, to the tops of the mountains; let his crops thrive like the forest of Lebanon; and let men sprout up in towns like country grass.*

17   *May his name be eternal; while the sun lasts, may his name endure; let men invoke his blessedness upon themselves; let all nations call him happy.*

18   *Blessed is God, the God of Israel, who alone does wondrous things;*

19   *Blessed is God's glorious name forever; God's glory fills the whole world. Amen and Amen.*

20   *End of the prayers of David son of Jesse.*

Will the Real King Please Stand Up?

To truly understand Psalm 72, we must answer a few questions: Who is speaking? About whom are they speaking? And on what occasion are they speaking? The easiest question to answer is the last one: This Psalm is a coronation poem marking the ascension of a new Israelite king.

The Psalm is built around the qualities the nation hopes the new king will embody. With an aspirational perspective, verses 1–7 speak of the king's righteousness in judgement. The king adjudicated many issues of justice and the poem prays for a king who will do so with wisdom and fairness. Verses 9–11 reflect on the king's greatness and the respect owed to him by foreign leaders. In verses 12–15, the Psalmist calls for the king's grace to be bestowed upon the poor and the needy in the kingdom.

In the ancient world the absolute power of the king was both a blessing and a curse. If the king was benevolent, then the people's needs were met, food was plentiful, and justice was equitably dispensed. But if the king was a despot, the people were overly taxed and suffered from reduced resources, unfair judgements, and economic conditions that increased their suffering. So, the coronation of a new king warranted praying that the new ruler should be kind, wise, and generous. We can say with certainty that Psalm 72 is just such a prayer.

But who is speaking, and about whom? These questions are up for debate.

The Psalm carries the headline "Of Solomon," and it is a reasonable conclusion that Solomon wrote this Psalm at the time of his own coronation. In this case, the header "Of Solomon" suggests a Psalm that is written *by* Solomon who may have used the song to reflect on the ideal qualities a king should possess, and to offer a plea to God to bestow those qualities upon him. Another possibility is that David wrote this Psalm on the occasion of his son's ascension to the throne. Seen in that light, the headline suggests it is a Psalm that speaks *about* Solomon.

Whether it is written by him or about him, Solomon is the "whom." And here is a linguistic element to note that further connects the Psalm to Solomon: In Hebrew, the name "Solomon," or Shlomo, derives from the word *shalom*, meaning *peace*. Verses 3 and 7 of our Psalm incorporate the word shalom. This may be a clever allusion to Solomon, the newly appointed king.

The last verses of our Psalm not only close out Psalm 72, but they also close out the third book of Psalms (on the five books of the Psalms, see "The Psalms: Five Books In One" on page 105). There are three notable elements found in this ending, one in each of the final three verses. Verse 17 proclaims, "let all nations call him happy." The use of the word "happy" (from the Hebrew root, *asher*) connects this to three other books in the collection, as all of the first four books end with a form of the word *asher*/happy. Verse 18 also repeats a familiar pattern. The first four books of the Psalms use a formulaic pronouncement: Blessed is God, Amen.

Most interesting is verse 19, which offers this declarative statement, "End of the prayers of David son of Jesse." This last verse of Psalm 72 is most certainly not part of the Psalm; rather, it is appended and meant as a conclusion to second

Book of Psalms. It seems to suggest that David wrote the Psalms until this point ('End of the prayers of David son of Jesse'), implying he did not write the ones that come after. This is strong evidence that an editorial hand was at work in assembling the Psalms and supports the scholarly conclusion that many of the Psalms were written by authors other than David.

A Hint of the Messiah

There is a Jewish tradition that finds a reference to the Messiah in verse 17: *May his name continue as long as the sun.* That Hebrew word for *continue, yinon,* is also a poetic name for the Messiah. Many liturgical poems, known as *piyutim,* refer to the Messiah as "Yinon." So it is that some rabbinic commentators understand our verse to be saying, "The Messiah's name is Yinon." By tradition, the Messiah will descend from the House of David, and these rabbinic voices see an embedded reference to this in our Psalm.

The Dreams of Solomon

Another part of the Bible shares a dream of Solomon's. In 1 Kings 3 verses 5–9, God appears to him in a dream and asks him his desires. Solomon asks for a discerning heart that can tell the difference between good and evil. God praises Solomon for not seeking personal wealth, and the dream sequence concludes with God saying,

> "Behold, I have done according to your words; I
> have given you a wise and understanding heart."

Much of the language found in that dream sequence is the same as here in Psalm 72. Some rabbinic commentators suggest that Psalm 72 is a poetic expansion of the very dream described in the Book of Kings. In both cases we find a foreshadowing of the great wisdom Solomon was known for.

SOUL STEPS

THE BOOK OF YOU

We discovered that the Psalm's headline, "Of Solomon," can mean either a Psalm written by or about Solomon. What if someone were to write about you?

Consider the life you live and the values you hold. If your life were a book, what review would others offer, and what review would you offer yourself?

What would others say about you and the values they observe you exhibiting?

What would you say about those same things?

What wisdom do you need to turn your life into a bestseller?

EMBEDDED MYSTERIES OF THE PSALMS

If only we understood everything in the Psalms; unfortunately, some words are a mystery. For example, three Psalms (39, 62, and 77) begin with a reference to *Yeduton*. Bible scholars debate whether this is the name of a specific Levite musician or a musical instruction. Many Psalms include a reference to *selah* which, as we noted elsewhere, is a musical cue for the musicians but exactly what it signals is lost to history. And as we see in Psalm 7, *shiggayon* might refer to a mistake for which David holds remorse; a musical instrument; or it might be an ecstatic poem (a 'rhapsody'). It can be frustrating to confront enigmatic words that confound us. However, when we consider that these 150 ancient poems are thousands of years old, perhaps it is more remarkable that we understand as much as we do. And we can even enjoy the mystery by reflecting on how the Psalm's message might change if the mysterious words were understood differently (for example, read Psalm 7 and ask yourself how the poem changes with each of the alternative understandings of *shiggayon*).

Psalm 85

¹ *For the Lead Musician. A Psalm of the sons of Korah.*

2 God, You will favor your land,
   You returned Jacob's fortune.

3 You have forgiven the iniquity of Your people,
   You have pardoned all their sin. Selah

4 You have withdrawn all Your anger;
   Return from Your rage.

5 Return us, O God of our salvation,
   And cause Your indignation toward us to cease.

6 Will You be angry with us forever?
   Prolong Your wrath for all generations?

7 Surely You will return us again,
   That Your people may rejoice in You.

8 Show us, O God, Your faithfulness;
   And grant us Your salvation.

9 Let me hear what God will speak;
   For God will speak peace unto the people, the faithful ones;
   But let them not return to folly.

10 Surely God's salvation is near to those that fear God;
   That God's glory may dwell in our land.

11 Love and truth meet;
   Righteousness and peace kiss.

12 Truth springs up from the land;
   And righteousness looks down from heaven.

13 God bestows bounty;
   And our land shall yield its produce.

14 *Righteousness shall go before God,*
   And walk in the way of God's steps.

When Life Gives Us Lemons and Lemonade

When we open the gift that is Psalm 85, inside the box are presents for the sensitive soul. Consider this gem that is neatly packaged inside:

> Love and truth meet;
> Righteousness and peace kiss

What a stunning turn of a phrase! Let's unpack the Psalm to better understand the treats that it holds.

Psalm 85 is both an ode to salvation already delivered and a plea for future salvation still needed. Some suggest that David wrote this poem amidst a severe drought, a condition in the ancient world that translated into food insecurity. As such, we catch the poet at a crossroads between appreciation for what was and anxiety for what may still come. In other words, this Psalm reflects the human condition where we routinely juggle joy and triumph while simultaneously managing anxiety and fear. David's words are a recognition that life is usually an exercise in mixed—and often conflicting—emotions.

Our Psalm opens with not one, but two introductions. The first is a musical instruction, *For the Lead Musician*, and the second one tells us the Psalm was written by—or for—the sons of Korach. There are eleven Psalms that mention the Sons of Korach in their opening instructions. What we don't know is if the Sons of Korach wrote the melodies for these eleven Psalms or if the melodies were written specifically for them to perform. That remains a mystery.

Those who recall their ancient Israelite history will remember that Korach and his sons rebelled against Moses and were swallowed up by the earth as punishment. The Book of Numbers clarifies that not all the Korachites died at that time. Not only did the family survive, as Levites they became a central part of the musical tradition in the Temple.

Repeating Words

In this Psalm, there are several words that repeat multiple times:

return	five times
salvation	three times
people	three times
righteousness	three times
justice	three times
land	four times

These key words, when taken together, summarize the poem's entire plotline: "You, God, returned to Your people before, and we hope You will return again now with new salvation. Your people will act with righteousness and justice; and may the land continue to produce food for the people."

Hidden Treasure 1

There are two buried treasures in Psalm 85, both in verse 12. The verse reads, *Emet me-eretz titzmakh—Truth will spring from the land.* If we take the first letter of the three Hebrew words in that phrase, those letters spell EMET. The Hebrew word for truth is *emet.*

Hidden Treasure 2

The second buried treasure in verse 12 is even more fun. If we write those three words, *Emet me-eretz titzmakh,* not in a linear sentence but stacked vertically, a hidden treat emerges. When written this way, if we read the new words that are formed in each column, the phrase that it spells is the same. *Emet me-eretz titzmakh!*

Did David intend these word plays? We can't know for sure, but we can enjoy them nonetheless.

א	מ	ת
מ	אר	צ
ת	צ	מח

SOUL STEPS

WHEN LIFE GIVES US LEMONS AND LEMONADE

We saw above that Psalm 85 was written as an expression of relief by David and his people upon overcoming challenging times, while also acknowledging there was a bumpy road ahead and that they were still afraid. Spend a few minutes reflecting on the messiness of life. What conflicting emotions do you feel when you are holding both relief and worry? During life's most confusing moments, reading Psalm 85 can reassure us that even King David experienced these bewildered emotions. With music and faith, he persevered.

PARTY LIKE THERE IS NO TOMORROW

Some Jews recite this Psalm the day after Yom Kippur in honor of an ancient custom. On Yom Kippur the High Priest had a once-a-year meeting with the Divine, inside the holiest space in the Temple: the Holy of Holies. The High Priest worried that if he failed to perform the rituals flawlessly, he might meet an untimely death. So, when he emerged successful in his tasks, it was his custom to throw a party the next day in celebration.

For those who observe Yom Kippur as a cleansing ritual for the soul, take a few minutes the next day and recite Psalm 85. Be mindful that had you not successfully come through the journey of soul-cleansing, you would be the same person you were a few days ago. Celebrate that you have grown, changed, and successfully exited the encounter as a new and better person.

LITERARY DEVICES IN THE PSALMS

Like most great literature, the Bible, including the Psalms, employs creative literary devices to capture our attention. Within the collection of Psalms there is storytelling and poetry, rhyming words and free flowing verse, words of warning and words of wisdom. Here is a quick review of some of the literary devices found within the Psalms:

ACROSTIC PSALMS

It is very common in liturgical material (Bible passages, prayers, religious poems) to find an alphabetical acrostic. Using the Hebrew alphabet to structure a written piece helps the listener or reader remember it. In the Psalms, we find complete acrostics, partial acrostics, and multiple acrostics (multiple verses for each letter of the alphabet). Some examples:

- Psalm 9 is a partial acrostic whose alphabet is slightly out of order.
- Psalm 25 is a complete acrostic with a couple of variations, such as missing one letter and doubling another one.
- Psalm 34 is complete except for a missing a verse for *vav*, the sixth letter of the Hebrew alphabet.

- Psalm 145 is missing the verse beginning with *nun*, the 14th letter of the Hebrew alphabet.
- Psalms 111 and 112 are complete acrostics but some letters are embedded within verses, meaning one verse may include two or three successive letters.
- Psalm 119 is a supersized acrostic with eight verses for each of the twenty-two Hebrew letters. Not surprising, it is also the longest Psalm.

RHYME

Some Psalms, like some poems, rhyme. Why? A rhyme structures a poem and can make it easier to memorize. It can add a musical lilt to the piece and that increases the reader's enjoyment, and rhyming words can create a sense of movement (a great example of this is Psalm 30). For millennia before the printing press was invented, no one owned personal scrolls or books, so rhyming verses and acrostics were employed as great memory aids.

GROUPED MANTRAS

It is common for a Psalm to ask a question and then to structure the rest of the Psalm as an answer to that question. Psalm 15, for example, asks the question, *God, who may abide in Your tent, who may dwell on Your holy mountain?* and then the next four verses each offer three answers to that question. In this way, the literary device serves as a pedagogic tool. By asking a question, the Psalm can then instruct us by way of the answers.

CONNECT THE DOTS

Whereas the other literary devices take place within a Psalm, sometimes we find a key word that links a series of Psalms. Psalms 103 and 104 contain the phrase *Barkhi nafshi*, or *Bless my soul, oh God*, five times. And the Halleluyah series—the final five Psalms of the entire collection—all begin and end with the word *Halleluyah*, or *Praise God*. And if that weren't enough, the word is used repeatedly within those five Psalms. How many times? Twenty-five! While this serves to connect the final five Psalms thematically, it is also a fitting conclusion to the entire collection of Psalms. The five books of praises to God—the Psalms—ends with thirty-five *halleluyahs*.

Psalm 104

1   Bless God, O my soul. God, my God, You are very great; clothed with glory and majesty.

2   You are clothed with light as a garment, You stretched out the heavens like a curtain.

3   Who lays the beams of Your upper chambers in the waters, makes the clouds Your chariot, walks upon the wings of the wind.

4   Who makes winds Your messengers, the flaming fire Your servants.

5   Who did establish the earth upon its foundations, That it should not ever totter.

6   You did cover the deep as with a garment; the waters stood above the mountains.

7   At Your rebuke they fled, at the sound of Your thunder they rushed away;

8   The mountains rose, the valleys sank; to the place You established for them.

9   You did set bounds which they should not pass over,
So that they never again cover the earth.

10   You sends springs into the valleys; they make their way between the mountains;

11   They give drink to every beast of the field, the wild asses quench their thirst.

12   The birds of the sky dwell beside them, they sing among the branches.

13   You water the mountains from Your upper chambers;
The earth is full of the fruit of Your works.

14 You make the grass grow for the cattle, and plants for the service of humankind;
To bring forth bread out of the earth,

15 And wine that cheers the human heart, oil that makes the face shine,
And bread that sustains life.

16 The trees of God have their fill, the cedars of Lebanon, which God planted;

17 Where birds make their nests; the stork has her home in the junipers.

19 The high mountains are for the wild goats; the rocks a refuge for badgers.

19 God made the moon to mark the seasons; the sun knows when to set.

20 You make darkness, and it is night, when all the beasts of the forest stir.

21 The young lions roar for prey, and seek their food from God.

22 When the sun arises, they come home, and couch in their dens.

23 Humans then go out to work and to labor until evening.

24 How many are Your works, O God! In wisdom You made them all;
The earth is full of Your creations.

25 There is the sea, vast and wide, with its creatures beyond number,
Living creatures, small and great.

26 There go the ships, and Leviathan, that You formed to sport with.

27 All of them look to You, to give them their food when it is due.

28 You give it to them, they gather it; You open Your hand, they are well satisfied.

29 Hide Your face, they are terrified; withdraw their breath, they perish, And return to dust.

30 Send forth Your breath, they are created; and You renew the face of the earth.

31 May the glory of God endure forever; let God rejoice in these works!

32 Who looks at the earth, and it trembles; God touches the mountains, and they smoke.

33 I will sing to God as long as I live; I will chant hymns to my God all my life.

34 May my prayer be pleasing to God; I will rejoice in God.

35 May sinners disappear from the earth, and let the wicked be no more.

36 Bless God, O my soul. Halleluyah.

The Creation Psalm

Many of us experience a sense of the Divine when we observe a beautiful sunset, the expansive ocean with its undulating waves, the intricacies of a rose with its silky petals, and so many other wonders of nature. Psalm 104 is a poem that praises the God of creation for the wonders of creation. The Psalm opens and closes with this simple and elegant command to the poet's soul: *Barkhi Nafshi/Bless God, O my soul.* And in the thirty-three verses between those opening and closing verses, there is beautiful poetic expression of the abundance of nature, the magnitude and power of nature, and praise for the God who alone could have created this magnificent natural world. For David (and many of us), when we encounter the awesomeness of nature, we genuinely feel like we are encountering an awesome God.

It is interesting that the Psalm approximately follows the pattern of creation found in the opening chapters of Genesis (though to be sure, there are a few deviations). Consider:

DAY OF CREATION IN TORAH	ELEMENTS CREATED IN THE TORAH	CREATION VERSES IN PSALM 104	ELEMENTS CREATED IN THE PSALM
1	Wind, light, darkness, water	1–6	Light, heavens, clouds, water, winds
2	Heavens, beginning formation of land	7–10	Dry land, sea, mountains
3	Dry land, sea, flora	10–18	Flora and fauna
4	Sun, moon, day, night	19–24	Sun, moon, day, night
5	The sea and all that is in it, birds	25–26	The sea and all that is in it
6	Fauna on the land, creation of humankind	27–30	Creation of humankind
7	God ceased creating and reflected on God's works	31–35	God rejoices in God's works

There is an interesting, albeit obscure, reference in verse 26. The verse speaks of a Leviathan, which is a mythical sea creature often depicted as a monster. The rabbis in the Talmud have two understandings about Leviathan.

One opinion is that it was a food source for the righteous in heaven, a delicacy served as a reward. A second opinion, based on our Psalm, is that God created this monster as a sparring partner (*that You formed to sport with*). From the Psalmist's perspective, Leviathan is a fearful creation for humans but no match for the powers of God.

In addition to praising the sheer beauty and magnitude of nature, the Psalmist offers us an important additional insight. The Psalm cues into the order and orderliness of nature. Most of the time nature cooperates. When it doesn't, the impacts can be catastrophic: hurricanes, floods, earthquakes, and droughts, for example. Psalm 104 praises God for the wonders of creation but also deeply appreciates the orderliness of creation. When nature acts as we expect it to—and need it to—that is worthy of soulful praise, so . . . *Bless God, O my soul.*

Back to the Future

The syntax in Psalm 104 is provocative. The poem switches between past, present, and future tenses repeatedly. Is this the sign of bad writing, or was David communicating something else? Actually, by switching between tenses, David cleverly underscores how creation is an ongoing process. The wonders of creation unfold every day: New life is birthed. Sunsets return. The earth, which has spun on its axis for millennia, will continue to do so tomorrow, next year, next century. This switching of tenses supports the rhythms of the natural world, something which David appreciated. In doing so, the Psalm beckons us to reflect on the continuum of creation, our own existence, and our place in between that which came before us and that which will follow us.

Multi-Sensory Magnificence

For the Psalmist, appreciating creation and the Creator was a whole body, multi-sensory experience. The poet declares, *I will sing to Adonai, I will offer meditations, I will rejoice,* and *I command my soul to bless God.* Truly his appreciation of the wonders of creation ran so deep that his soul, his body, and his senses all were inspired to offer praise.

SOUL STEPS

WORSHIPPING WITH OUR WHOLE BODY

In Psalms 103 and 104 we find the phrase *Barkhi nafshi/Bless God, O my soul* a total of five times. As noted above, appreciating creation and the Creator was a whole body experience for the poet. Is there ever a time when you are so filled with enthusiasm, love, or joy for something that your words are not nearly enough to express it? What additional mechanisms do you use to express your feelings at those moments? Do you turn to creative endeavors to channel these peak emotions?

A WEEK TO NOTICE THE WORLD

We learned above that Psalm 104 parallels the week of creation in the opening chapter of Genesis. In his poetic reflection on the majesty of the natural world, David seeks to inspire us to notice and appreciate the very same created world he witnessed.

Spend a week contemplating the creations around you. Starting on Sunday, follow the Psalm's rendering of creation in the chart above and each day spend a few minutes reflecting on its unique creations. Begin by paying attention to those elements. Think about how you interact with them and how your world would be different without them. Then, on Shabbat, the seventh day of your "week of noticing the world," find a natural space that inspires your soul and reread Psalm 104. Has the Psalm changed for you? Have you changed from when you first read it?

Psalms 113–118

PSALM 113

1 Halleluyah. O servants of God, give praise; praise the name of God.

2 Let the name of God be blessed now and forever.

3 From east to west the name of God is praised.

4 God is exalted above all nations; whose glory is above the heavens.

5 Who is like God our God, who, enthroned on high,

6 sees what is below, in heaven and on earth?

7 God raises the poor from the dust, lifts up the needy from the refuse heap

8 to set them with the great, with the great ones of God's people.

9 God sets the childless woman among her household as a happy mother of children. Halleluyah.

PSALM 114

1 When Israel went forth from Egypt, the house of Jacob from a people of strange speech,

2 Judah became God's holy one; Israel, God's dominion.

3 The sea saw them and fled, the Jordan ran backward,

4 mountains skipped like rams, hills like sheep.

5 What alarmed you, O sea, that you fled, Jordan, that you ran backward,

6 mountains, that you skipped like rams, hills, like sheep?

7 Tremble, O earth, at the presence of God, at the presence of the God of Jacob,

⁸   who turned the rock into a pool of water, the flinty rock into
    a fountain.

PSALM 115

¹   Not to us, O God, not to us but to Your name bring glory for
    the sake of Your love and Your faithfulness.

³   Let the nations not say, "Where, now, is their God?"
    when our God is in heaven and accomplishes all that God
    wills.

⁴   Their idols are silver and gold, the work of men's hands.

⁵   They have mouths, but cannot speak, eyes, but cannot see;

⁶   they have ears, but cannot hear, noses, but cannot smell;

⁷   they have hands, but cannot touch, feet, but cannot walk;
    they can make no sound in their throats.

⁸   Those who fashion them, all who trust in them, shall become
    like them.

⁹   O Israel, trust in God! their help and shield.

¹⁰ O house of Aaron, trust in God! their help and shield.

¹¹ O you who fear God, trust in God! their help and shield.

¹² God is mindful of us. God will bless us; God will bless the
    house of Israel;
    God will bless the house of Aaron;

¹³ God will bless those who fear God, small and great alike.

¹⁴ May God increase your numbers, yours and your children's
    also.

¹⁵ May you be blessed by God, Maker of heaven and earth.

¹⁶ The heavens belong to God, but the earth God gave over to
    humans.

¹⁷ The dead cannot praise God, nor any who go down into
    silence.

¹⁸ But we will bless God now and forever. Halleluyah.

PSALM 116

1 I love God who hears my voice, my pleas;
2 for God turns an ear to me whenever I call.
3 The bonds of death encompassed me; the torments of Sheol overtook me.

I came upon trouble and sorrow

4 and I invoked the name of God, "O God, save my life!"
5 God is gracious and beneficent; our God is compassionate.
6 God protects the simple; I was brought low and God saved me.
7 Be at rest, once again, O my soul, for God has been good to you.
8 You have delivered me from death, my eyes from tears, my feet from stumbling.
9 I shall walk before God in the lands of the living.
10 I trust [in God]; out of great suffering I spoke
11 and said rashly, "All men are false."
12 How can I repay God for all God's bounties to me?
13 I raise the cup of deliverance and invoke the name of God.
14 I will pay my vows to God in the presence of all God's people.
15 The death of the faithful ones is grievous in God's sight.
16 O God, I am Your servant, Your servant, the son of Your maidservant; You have undone the cords that bound me.
17 I will sacrifice a thank offering to You and invoke the name of God.
18 I will pay my vows to God in the presence of all God's people,
19 in the courts of the house of God, in the midst of Jerusalem. Halleluyah.

PSALM 117

1 Praise God, all you nations; extol God, all you peoples,
2 for great is God's steadfast love toward us; the faithfulness of God endures forever. Halleluyah.

PSALM 118

1 Praise God, who is good, God's steadfast love is eternal.

2 Let Israel declare, "God's steadfast love is eternal."

3 Let the house of Aaron declare, "God's steadfast love is eternal."

4 Let those who fear God declare, "God's steadfast love is eternal."

5 In distress I called on God; God answered me and brought me relief.

6 God is on my side, I have no fear; what can man do to me?

7 With God on my side as my helper, I will see the downfall of my foes.

8 It is better to take refuge in God than to trust in mortals;

9 it is better to take refuge in God than to trust in the great.

10 All nations have beset me; by the name of God I will surely cut them down.

11 They beset me, they surround me; by the name of God I will surely cut them down.

12 They have beset me like bees; they shall be extinguished like burning thorns; by the name of God I will surely cut them down.

13 You pressed me hard, I nearly fell; but God helped me.

14 God is my strength and might; Who has become my deliverance.

15 The tents of the victorious resound with joyous shouts of deliverance,
    "The right hand of God is triumphant!

16 The right hand of God is exalted! The right hand of God is triumphant!"

17 I shall not die but live and proclaim the works of God.

18 God punished me severely, but did not hand me over to death.

19 Open the gates of victory for me that I may enter them and praise God.

20 This is the gateway to God—the victorious shall enter through it.

21 I praise You, for You have answered me, and have become my deliverance.

22 The stone that the builders rejected has become the chief cornerstone.

23 This is God's doing; it is marvelous in our sight.

24 This is the day that God has made—let us exult and rejoice on it.

25 O God, deliver us! O God, let us prosper!

26 May they who enter be blessed in the name of God; we bless you from the House of God.

27 God is God; Who has given us light; bind the festival offering to the horns of the altar with cords.

28 You are my God and I will praise You; You are my God and I will extol You.

29 Praise God for God is good, Whose steadfast love is eternal.

The Egyptian Praise

Psalms 113–118 are treated as a unit by Jewish tradition and became known as *Hallel Ha-mitzri*, the *Egyptian Praise* or the *Egyptian Hallel*. An odd name, considering that Egypt is not being praised. Rather, God is praised for freeing the Israelites from Egypt (Psalm 114:1 specifically references this). Though officially called *Hallel Ha-mitzri*, in synagogues it is often simply called *Hallel*, or *Praise*. How often? Hallel is recited in synagogues the world over on most major Jewish festivals, the monthly observance of the new moon, which begins each new month, Israel Independence Day, Hanukkah, and at the Passover *Seder*.

What Is Being Praised in Hallel?

The praises are universal and particular, national and individual. At times they recognize God for specific acts of redemption and salvation; at other times, the praises are for general Divine kindness and grace. Consider the many praises within Hallel:

> In **Psalm 113**, God's Name; God exalted above all creations; God's compassion to lift up the downtrodden and support barren woman.

> In **Psalm 114**, Israel's successful departure from Egypt; God parted the Sea, showing dominion over the natural world, and provisioned the Israelites with water in the desert.

In **Psalm 115**, while idols of silver and gold have no power, praise is offered to God who is the source Israel turns to for help. And praise to God for bestowing the blessings of abundance and progeny.

In **Psalm 116**, praises for personal healing are given to the Psalmist amidst a life-threatening saga. It presents a simple, yet profound truth: only the living can praise God. Salvation from near death is cause for praise. The Psalm ends with a pledge to give a thanksgiving offering at the Temple in Jerusalem.

In **Psalm 117**, the shortest Psalm of all, there are more reasons for praise than there are verses–three reasons to praise in only two short verses. Referencing the universality of God's sovereignty, the nations should praise God; God's love is highlighted as praiseworthy, as is God's enduring faithfulness to the Children of Israel.

In **Psalm 118**, which was likely recited by those going up to the Temple in Jerusalem with a thanksgiving offering, they are thankful for God's goodness and eternal love; for God who answers distress calls of the soul, offers protection from enemies, and provides strength and deliverance.

In Psalms 113–118, praise abounds. There is a multitude of praise; an abundance of praise; an enormity of praise; an overflowing fount of praise! And if all the praises within these Psalms were not enough, in some synagogue communities the congregation responds, "Halleluyah, praise God," after each verse recited by the prayer leader. One hundred and twenty-three halleluyahs!

The Passover Connection

In addition to referencing the Exodus from Egypt in Psalm 114:1, these Psalms carry connections to Passover.

- The *Mishnah*[1] (part of the Talmud) teaches that Hallel was recited when arranging for the paschal lamb, the Passover offering that was central to the holiday observance in the days of the Temple.
- Nowadays, though we no longer offer a paschal sacrifice, instead we recite Hallel at the Passover *Seder* in praise of the liberation our ancestors experienced as they departed Egypt.
- In Psalm 118, we read, *In distress, I called to God who answered me with liberation.* The word for *distress*, *meitzar*, is related to the word *mitzrayim*, or *Egypt*, which literally means "a constricted place." Egypt was physically constricting and personal distress is emotionally constricting. Passover celebrates liberation from a constricted place, and Psalm 118 offers praises to God who answers the cry of the constricted soul.
- Psalm 118 directly quotes the Song at the Sea, sung by Moses and Miriam in joyous celebration. Found in both Exodus 15:2 and Psalm 118:14, we read, *Ah-zi ve-zimrat yah; va'yehi li le-yeshua,* or *God is my strength and song; God is my salvation.*

[1] Mishnah Pesahim 5:7

Indeed, the great act of liberation from slavery in Egypt is celebrated in this magnificent collection of Psalms of praise.

Tidbits from Hallel's History

The Egyptian Hallel is among the very oldest pieces of liturgy we possess. From ancient rabbinic literature, we know it was recited at the Second Temple and with great fanfare. Choirs of Levites performed the Hallel, accompanied by an orchestra of flutes. All this was in the presence of masses of pilgrims who descended on Jerusalem for the occasion. No doubt the recitation of Hallel was an ecstatic experience. There is a direct link between its inclusion in the Second Temple rites and synagogues today reciting Hallel on the holidays. In fact, in most synagogues when Hallel is chanted, it is done so with much singing and spirited melodies. Perhaps not quite the ecstatic experience of the Second Temple, but a highpoint nonetheless.

There are many Jewish legends about when Hallel was first recited. Some legends ascribe it to myriad Biblical figures who escaped danger: Joshua, Deborah, or even Esther and Mordechai. Another tradition suggests that it was offered by Moses and the Israelites as they fled Egypt. With Pharaoh's army chasing them from behind and the Red Sea in front of them, they chanted the Hallel, beseeching God to part the Red Sea. In this version of the story, it's interesting to note that on some days of Passover, we recite a truncated version of Hallel. Why? According to another Jewish legend, though the Egyptians were Israel's oppressors, they were still human beings who lost their lives when they drowned in the Red Sea, and it was deemed inappropriate to celebrate this loss of life by chanting Hallel and celebrating on the holiday which included their demise. So, the tradition developed to diminish the recitation of Hallel on some of the days of Passover.

Simply stated, Hallel is a feel-good experience. Because of its words, messages, and the catchy tunes which usually accompany it, it is difficult to encounter a Hallel service without being uplifted. And for that, we say, "Halleluyah!"

SOUL STEPS

THE JOY OF PERSONAL RELEASE

Above we discovered the word *mitzrayim*, or Egypt, is from the same word that means *constricted place*. And it was noted that Egypt was a *physically* constricting place for the Israelite slaves, while distress for us today tends to be *emotionally* constricting.

Think about something that is or was distressing you. In what ways does the distress impact your body, spirit, and emotional wellbeing? What does it feel like when you succeed in freeing yourself from that distress? Depending on the gravity of the burden, it may even feel like the parting of the Red Sea and arriving safely to the other side . . . to a place of freedom. Now, or in the future, when your soul is overly burdened, reciting Hallel—or singing it, if you can familiarize yourself with its melodies—may lift your spirits as it has to so many over the millennia.

A MULTITUDE OF GRATITUDE

This gratitude exercise can be enjoyed by anyone: couples, families (the many ways that is defined), friends, siblings.

Begin by asking each participant to prepare a list of blessings they are grateful for and the ways they experience these gifts in their lives. Invite each participant to share their list, and after each expression of gratitude, guide the group to respond, "Halleluyah."

This is also a meaningful way to honor someone—a birthday celebrant, a college graduate, a loved one who has accomplished a meaningful achievement—by asking participants to create lists of qualities they appreciate about the honoree. As they read their lists aloud, after each one, the group responds, "Halleluyah."

THE MUSIC OF THE GREAT TEMPLE

It is hard for us to imagine the grandeur of the Great Temple in Jerusalem. Perched high on a hilltop, it was an imposing structure both physically and culturally. Every facet of ancient Jewish life – ritual worship, legal adjudication, political structure, and religious stricture – was centered at the Temple. And amidst this frenzy of activities, the musical arts were prominent.

Consider the word 'psalm.' It comes from the Latin word 'psallo' meaning "to play on or to sing to a string instrument." The Levites – members of the Priestly clan – were responsible for performing the music and many Psalms are the musical scores they followed. There are musical instructions, references to specific musical instruments, and even dedications to specific Levites singled out for their musical excellence.

Here are a few examples:

The term '*selah*' appears often throughout the Psalms. We know it is a musical cue of some kind, though its meaning is unknown.

Examples of musical instruments mentioned are *higgayon*, a kind of harp; *nigginot, a* stringed instrument; and *shminit,* from the word 'eight,' which might suggest it was an 8-stringed instrument capable of playing a full octave. Also, cymbals, flutes, and shofar (a ram's horn).

Within the Psalms are references to 'The Conductor'; 'For the Leader on Instrumental Music'; and, of course, the maestros of Temple music, 'The Levites.'

Literally and figuratively, the Psalms were music to the ancient Israelites' ears...and hearts.

Psalm 120–134

PSALM 120

1 A Song of Ascents. In my distress I called to God and God answered me.

2 God, save me from treacherous lips, from a deceitful tongue!

3 What can you profit, what can you gain, O deceitful tongue?

4 A warrior's sharp arrows, with hot coals of broom-wood.

5 Woe is me, that I live with Meshech, that I dwell among the clans of Kedar.

6 Too long have I dwelt with those who hate peace.

7 I am all peace; but when I speak, they are for war.

PSALM 121

1 A Song of Ascents. I turn my eyes to the mountains; from where will my help come?

2 My help comes from God, maker of heaven and earth.

3 God will not let your foot give way; your guardian will not slumber;

4 See, the guardian of Israel neither slumbers nor sleeps!

5 God is your guardian, God is your protection at your right hand.

6 By day the sun will not strike you, nor the moon by night.

7 God will guard you from all harm; God will guard your life.

8 God will guard your going and coming now and forever.

PSALM 122

1 A Song of Ascents; of David.

² *I rejoiced when they said unto me: "Let us go to the house of God."*

³ *Our feet stood within your gates, O Jerusalem;*

⁴ *Jerusalem, built up, A city knit together;*

⁵ *To which the tribes would make pilgrimage, the tribes of God,*

⁶ *As was enjoined upon Israel, To give thanks to the name of God.*

⁷ *There the thrones of judgment stood, the thrones of the house of David.*

⁸ *Pray for the peace of Jerusalem; May those that love you be at peace.*

⁹ *Peace be within your walls, And prosperity within your palaces.*

¹⁰ *For the sake of my brethren and companions, I pray for your wellbeing;*

¹¹ *For the sake of the house of our God I seek your good.*

PSALM 123

¹ *A Song of Ascents. To You, enthroned in heaven, I turn my eyes.*

² *As the eyes of slaves follow their master's hand, as the eyes of a slave-girl follow the hand of her mistress, so our eyes are toward God our God, awaiting favor.*

³ *Show us favor, O God, show us favor! We have had more than enough of contempt.*

⁴ *Long enough have we endured the scorn of the complacent, the contempt of the haughty.*

PSALM 124

¹ *A Song of Ascents. Of David. Were it not for God, who was on our side, let Israel now declare,*

2   *were it not for God, who was on our side when men assailed us,*

3   *they would have swallowed us alive in their burning rage against us;*

4   *the waters would have carried us off, the torrent would have swept over us;*

5   *over us would have swept the seething waters.*

6   *Blessed is God, who did not let us be ripped apart by their teeth.*

7   *We are like a bird escaped from the fowler's trap; the trap broke and we escaped.*

8   *Our help is the name of God, maker of heaven and earth.*

PSALM 125

1   A Song of Ascents. Those who trust in God are like Mount Zion that cannot be removed, enduring forever.

2   As the mountains surround Jerusalem, so God enfolds the people now and forever.

3   The scepter of the wicked shall never rest upon the land allotted to the righteous, that the righteous not set their hand to wrongdoing.

4   Do good, O God, to those who are good and upright in heart.

5   But those who in their crookedness act corruptly, let God make them go the way of evildoers. May it be well with Israel!

PSALM 126

1   A Song of Ascents.

2   When God returned us to Zion, We were like dreamers.

3   Then our mouths will be filled with laughter, And our tongues with songs of joy;

4   Then they shall say among the nations: "God has done great things for them."

5   God will do great things for us; We will rejoice.

6   Turn our captivity, O God, Like the streams in the Negev.

7   They who sow in tears, Shall reap in joy.

8   They who go along weeping, bearing a bag of seed,

9   shall come home with joy, carrying their sheaves.

PSALM 127

1   A Song of Ascents. Of Solomon. Unless God builds the house, its builders labor in vain on it; unless God watches over the city, the watchman keeps vigil in vain.

2   In vain do you rise early and stay up late, you who toil for the bread you eat; God provides as much for God's loved ones while they sleep.

3   Children are a heritage of God; the fruit of the womb is a reward.

4   Like arrows in the hand of a warrior so are children born in one's youth.

5   Happy is the one who fills his quiver with them; they shall not be put to shame when they contend with the enemy in the gate.

PSALM 128

1   A Song of Ascents. Happy are all who fear God, who follow God's ways.

2   You shall enjoy the fruit of your labors; you shall be happy and you shall prosper.

3   Your wife shall be like a fruitful vine within your house; your children, olive saplings around your table.

4   So shall the one who fears God be blessed.

5   May God bless you from Zion; may you share the prosperity of Jerusalem all the days of your life,

6   and live to see your children's children. May all be well with Israel!

PSALM 129

1 A Song of Ascents. Since my youth they have often assailed me, let Israel now declare,

2 since my youth they have often assailed me, but they have never overcome me.

3 Plowmen plowed across my back; they made long furrows.

4 God, the righteous one, has snapped the cords of the wicked.

5 Let all who hate Zion fall back in disgrace.

6 Let them be like grass on roofs that fades before it can be pulled up,

7 that affords no handful for the reaper, no armful for the gatherer of sheaves,

8 no exchange with passersby: "The blessing of God be upon you." "We bless you by the name of God."

PSALM 130

1 A Song of Ascents. Out of the depths I call You, O God.

2 God, listen to my cry; let Your ears be attentive to my plea for mercy.

3 If You keep account of sins, O God, who will survive?

4 Yours is the power to forgive so that You may be held in awe.

5 I look to God; my soul waits; I await God's word.

6 I am more eager for God than watchmen for the morning, watchmen for the morning.

7 Israel, wait for God; for with God is steadfast love and great power to redeem.

8 It is God who will redeem Israel from all their iniquities.

PSALM 131

1 A Song of Ascents. Of David. O God, my heart is not proud nor my look haughty; I do not aspire to great things or to what is beyond me;

2 but I have taught myself to be contented like a weaned child with its mother; like a weaned child am I in my mind.

3 Israel, wait for God now and forever.

PSALM 132

1 A Song of Ascents. O God, remember in David's favor his extreme self-denial,

2 how he swore to God, vowed to the Mighty One of Jacob,

3 "I will not enter my house, nor will I mount my bed,

4 I will not give sleep to my eyes, or slumber to my eyelids

5 until I find a place for God, an abode for the Mighty One of Jacob."

6 We heard it was in Ephrath; we came upon it in the region of Jaar.

7 Let us enter God's abode, bow at God's footstool.

8 Advance, O God, to Your resting-place, You and Your mighty Ark!

9 Your priests are clothed in triumph; Your loyal ones sing for joy.

10 For the sake of Your servant David do not reject Your anointed one.

11 God swore to David a firm oath and will not turn from it, "One of your own issue I will set upon your throne.

12 If your sons keep My covenant and My decrees that I teach them, then their sons also, to the end of time, shall sit upon your throne."

13 For God has chosen Zion; desired it for God's seat.

14 "This is my resting-place for all time; here I will dwell, for I desire it.

15 I will amply bless its store of food, give its needy their fill of bread.

16 I will clothe its priests in victory, its loyal ones shall sing for joy.

17 *There I will make a horn sprout for David; I have prepared a lamp for My anointed one.*

18 *I will clothe his enemies in disgrace, while on him his crown shall sparkle."*

PSALM 133

1 *A Song of Ascents. Of David. How good and how pleasant it is that brothers dwell together.*

2 *It is like fine oil on the head running down onto the beard, the beard of Aaron, that comes down over the collar of his robe;*

3 *like the dew of Hermon that falls upon the mountains of Zion. There God commanded the blessing of everlasting life.*

PSALM 134

1 *A Song of Ascents. Now bless God, all you servants of God who stand nightly in the house of God.*

2 *Lift your hands toward the sanctuary and bless God.*

3 *May God, maker of heaven and earth, bless you from Zion.*

Songs of Ascent

What's up with Psalms 120–134? Actually, quite a lot. These fifteen Psalms all begin with a form of the phrase *Shir Ha-ma'a lot*, or A Song of Ascent. And so we ask, who is ascending, and to where are they going? Rabbis and scholars throughout the centuries have offered many suggestions:

- Songs sung by pilgrims bringing their first fruits to the Temple on the three pilgrimage festivals (Passover, Shavuot, and Sukkot).
- Songs composed for the festive *Simkhat Beit Hasho'eva*, or Water Libation Ceremony, held in ancient times on Sukkot.
- Songs sung by the captives returning from Babylonian exile.
- Musical compositions wherein the singers' voices ascended in volume.
- Fifteen Psalms sung by the Levites who needed to ascend fifteen steps in the Temple en route to their ritual functions.
- Songs recited at the Temple altar while offering the *Korban Olah*, or the *Ascending Sacrifice*, whose sweet smells were meant to go up to God.

While we can't know for sure, the most likely explanations are the first two: They were songs sung by pilgrims bringing their first fruits and lyrical supplications for the Water Libation celebration. History assembled these fifteen Psalms consecutively, in contrast to Psalms with the same introductory label that are sprinkled throughout the Book of Psalms. Because these fifteen Psalms appear together, contain many similar thematic elements, and were almost certainly written and chanted by a group of worshippers at the Great Temple in Jerusalem, let's explore them here as a unit—while still shining a light on some charming and unique elements specific to individual Psalms.

The fifteen Songs of Ascent are grouped around five themes:[1]

Psalms 120, 123, 130	A call for salvation from hard times
Psalms 121, 133, 134	An appreciation for life's blessings
Psalms 122, 126, 132	A return to or an appreciation for Jerusalem
Psalms 124, 125, 129	Faith that God will provide protection
Psalms 127, 128, 131	Ethical lessons that result from living with good values

It is noteworthy that in each of the fifteen Psalms, one or more of the following themes is referenced:

A plea before God

Mountains

A house

Zion

Jerusalem

The heavens

Israel

Let's explore two of the Songs of Ascent in depth.

[1] Adapted from The Psalms, Mosad Harav Kook edition, 1990, Jerusalem.

PSALM 122: A LOVE LETTER TO JERUSALEM

In the introduction to the Songs of Ascent, we discover that some of these celebrate a pilgrimage to Jerusalem. Psalm 122 communicates the pure joy of the pilgrim recounting his journey. In nine short verses, we feel what he felt and we sense his unbridled enthusiasm. The poet is recounting the journey, beginning with the moment the trip was announced:

> I was overjoyed when they told me we were going to the House of God.

It is as though he is sitting around his dining room table with friends and sharing his vacation travelogue. His memories are vivid, and his excitement is palpable as he so vibrantly regales his guests with stories of his epic pilgrimage. We can easily understand his reflections and appreciate his exuberance:

> Our feet stood within your gates, O Jerusalem.

After our long journey, a journey filled with anticipation, we finally arrived, and I was overcome with the realization that I was actually standing in Jerusalem.

> Jerusalem, built up, a city knit together.

Though I didn't know what to expect, I was pleased to find a Jerusalem well established, filled with thriving neighborhoods one after the other.

> To which the tribes would make pilgrimage, the tribes of God,

> As was enjoined upon Israel, To give thanks to
> the name of God.

Imagine how awe-inspiring it was to be in the very same place where our ancestors who settled the land of Israel stood, to be in the same spot to which they made pilgrimage.

> There the thrones of judgment stood, the thrones
> of the house of David.

I was overcome to look upon the Temple Mount knowing that right here is where God established the kingdom for Israelites, then and now.

> Pray for the peace of Jerusalem; May those that
> love you be at peace.
> Peace be within your walls, and prosperity
> within your palaces.
> For the sake of my brethren and companions, I
> pray for your wellbeing.

I was so moved by it all that before I departed for home, I uttered a prayer. I prayed that Jerusalem would know peace. I prayed that those who love her will have peace. That there will be peace within the city, within her institutions, and I prayed that our compatriots, the residents of Jerusalem, will have prosperity and thrive.

It is safe to assume that the pilgrim was bringing his first fruits to the Temple. That was the purpose of the pilgrimage. Yet, there is no mention of the offering of the fruits. What could explain this omission? One answer might be that the offering of the produce required a journey not everyone could undertake. If one was not able to travel to Jerusalem, they sent their gifts with others to deliver on their behalf. So whereas the first fruits offering was a regular occurrence whether in person or by proxy, this poem celebrates the very special event of the journey itself. This year, the journey was the destination!

Who Wrote Psalm 122?

The Introduction to this book noted that David likely did not write all the Psalms. Psalm 122 is one example. How do we know that David couldn't have written this Psalm, in which the writer describes the Temple? Because the Temple wasn't built yet—David had a vision for its creation, but it was his son, King Solomon, who built it. Instead of being written by David, the first verse, which references David, does so as a way of dedicating the Psalm to him.

While we don't know who wrote Psalm 122, we do know the author was a devout Israelite pilgrim, overflowing with joy, and a gifted writer who channeled his emotions into a love letter to Jerusalem.

Little City, Many Attributes

Within this relatively short Psalm, many are the attributes of Jerusalem. Jerusalem is the *House of God*, a *city knit together*, the *throne of judgement*, the *House of David*, and the *House of our God*. It is as if our joyful pilgrim on his long-awaited trip to Jerusalem, made sure to see all the sights and experience everything the big city had to offer.

SOUL STEPS

CELEBRATING OUR OWN PILGRIMAGE TO JERUSALEM

The pilgrimage to Jerusalem included great pageantry. The people of each town or region journeyed together in a festive parade, led by a bull with gold-gilded horns. As they neared the city, they called out the very same words recorded in Verse 1 of our Psalm,

> I rejoiced when they said unto me: "Let us go to the house of God."

They sent messengers ahead to announce the arrival of their regional delegation, and when they were about to enter the city, they proclaimed the very words found in verse two,

> Our feet stand within your gates, O Jerusalem.

There was a wonderful interplay between the travelers and the citizens of Jerusalem, who would turn out to welcome and serenade the pilgrims.

If you are fortunate to travel to Israel, allow yourself the time to process your feelings about your pilgrimage. As you walk the streets of Jerusalem, consider who might have walked in the very place you find yourself. King Solomon? The Prophet Isaiah? Rabbis Akiva and Hillel? The pilgrim who authored this Psalm? Like our Psalmist did in verse four, imagine that you are the latest pilgrim in an ancient chain linking the Jewish People—across thousands of years and around the world—to this magical and mystical place, Jerusalem.

Upon your departure, write a prayer for Jerusalem. What do you wish for her, for her residents, and for all who hold her in their hearts?

Imagine if the one aspiration you most desire actually materialized. Would it feel surreal and unbelievable? Might you sense unbridled joy and maybe even a bit of trepidation? Psalm 126 is an expression of the Psalmist's emotions confronting the realization of his deepest held dream: the return to Jerusalem after exile and slavery.

In 587 BCE, the Babylonians conquered Israel, destroyed the Temple in Jerusalem, and carted off a segment of the nation into exile. This was a national catastrophe of the worst kind. Independence and self-governance were lost and the entire system of worship was destroyed along with the Temple compound. The people of Israel were despondent and in shock. For the exiles who spent fifty years traumatized by the Babylonian expulsion and servitude, their highest aspiration as individuals and as a nation was to return to Jerusalem to rebuild the Temple.

With that historical background, we can understand the conflicting emotions of the exiles. They had a deep longing for the return to and restoration of Jerusalem and the Temple. Yet, lest they be bitterly disappointed, they dared not allow themselves to expect it. Psalm 126 reflects both those realities: the tempering of hopes and expectations alongside overwhelming joy.

Even the language and syntax of Psalm 126 reflect these contrasting emotions: Due to a quirk of Hebrew syntax, some Hebrew words can be read either as past tense or future tense. Thus, Psalm 126 is either a celebration of a return that has already happened or a prayer for future restoration. The case for the poet celebrating his dream being realized is best seen in verses 1 and 2:

1. A Song of Ascents.
2. When God returned us to Zion, We were like dreamers.

And the case for this being aspirational is clear in verses 3 and 4:

1. Then our mouths will be filled with laughter, And our tongues with songs of joy;
2. Then they shall say among the nations: "God has done great things for them."

This linguistic toggling between future hope and real-time gratitude has the effect of emphasizing the conflicting emotions one feels when actually realizing a still unfathomable dream. The dreamer can hardly believe it has finally come true and the text cleverly captures this duality.

Yet another aspect of the dreamer's experience is reflected through the language of the Psalm. Sometimes in life we are in a state of disbelief, asking ourselves, *Did that really happen?* We rely on others to confirm our perception. The poet notes that the other nations are speaking of the great and wondrous return from exile (verse 2). Only then does he begin to believe that his dreams are coming true (verse 3). It is as if the poet were saying, "We didn't believe it ourselves until we heard others talking about the great things God did for us. Apparently, our dreams did come true; we are returning to Jerusalem to rebuild the Temple."

The Emotion of Poetry
This relatively short poem relies on the literary device of repeating words and themes that we highlighted in the introduction to the fifteen Songs of Ascent. Underscoring the

Psalm's central theme of the unimaginable release from exile and return to Jerusalem, verses 4–6 each present a metaphor for experiencing something great and unexpected. The reference to *the streams of the Negev* cues into the natural phenomenon of flash floods that regularly occur in the Negev, the southern desert region in Israel. When a storm occurs, streams that are typically dry or meandering can quickly turn into raging rivers.

The next two verses rely on the joyful turn of events when one sows a field with the lowest of expectations for its success and yet, months later, reaps vast quantities with joyous tears in the eyes. As the streams of the Negev gushed forth, and so too did our fields turn lush with produce, and so did the exiles flow from Babylon back to Jerusalem:

> *We were like dreamers.*
> *Our mouths were filled with laughter, And our tongues with songs of joy . . .*

Food for Thought

Psalm 126 has an extremely prominent role in Jewish life. It is sung by Jews in every corner of the globe as the introduction to *Birkhat Hamazon*, or grace after meals, at every Shabbat and festival meal. The origins of this custom are twofold. First, it seems to be based on the Zohar, the primary text of *Kabbalah*, or Jewish mysticism. The Zohar teaches,[2] "Whoever is enjoying their table and enjoying these foods should be sure to mention and express concern for the holiness of the Holy Land, and for the Temple which was destroyed."

Second, there is a longstanding Jewish custom that one's Shabbat table serves as a replacement altar for the destroyed Temple. Just as the Psalm reflects the hopes, dreams, and

[2] Zohar, Terumah 157a

utter joy of the returning exiles from Babylon, when we sing its words at our "altars"–our festive tables–we are expressing appreciation for the abundance of food we have and the nurturing company of family and friends around us.

SOUL STEPS

IMAGINING THE UNIMAGINABLE

What is the best thing that ever happened to you in your life? Consider the magnitude of its impact. Did you long for it or was it a surprise? Create a list of words you would use to describe it and its impact on your life. Parents, you can adapt this exercise to help their children develop intuition: Ask your child to think about something wonderful they wish for. Have them imagine what it would feel like to have that dream come true.

HISTORICAL REFERENCES IN THE PSALMS

We know that poets and songwriters often find creative inspiration from historical events. The Psalms are no different. Many Psalms allude to historical events found elsewhere in the Bible, experienced personally by David, or major historical events in the life of the nation. For example, Psalm 3 speaks of a rebellion against King David by his own son, Abshalom, and Psalm 126 reflects on the end of the Babylonian exile and the return of the captives to Jerusalem in the sixth century BCE. Some historical events are referenced multiple times, such as the Israelite exodus from Egypt, which is mentioned in no fewer than twenty Psalms!

Historians benefit from these references because two different texts that speak about the same event can be used to confirm the accuracy of the narrative. Likewise, these references can present challenges if the historical records differ. But one thing is certain: If a Psalm speaks of an historical event, we know it was an impactful and meaningful experience for the Psalm's author.

Psalms 135–136

PSALM 135

1 Halleluyah. Praise the name of God; give praise, you servants of God

2 who stand in the house of God, in the courts of the house of our God.

3 Praise God, for God is good; sing hymns to God's name, for it is pleasant.

4 For God has chosen Jacob, Israel, as God's treasured possession.

5 For I know that God is great, that our God is greater than all Gods.

6 Whatever God desires God does in heaven and earth, in the seas and all the depths.

7 God makes clouds rise from this end of the earth; God makes lightning for the rain; God releases wind from God's vaults.

8 God struck down the first-born of Egypt, man and beast alike;
God sent signs and portents against Egypt, against Pharaoh and all his servants;

9 God struck down many nations and slew numerous kings—

10 Sihon, king of the Amorites, Og, king of Bashan, and all the royalty of Canaan—

11 and gave their lands as a heritage, as a heritage to the people Israel.
O God, Your name endures forever, Your fame, O God, through all generations;

12 for God will champion His people, and obtain satisfaction for God's servants.

13 The idols of the nations are silver and gold, the work of men's hands.

14 They have mouths, but cannot speak; They have eyes, but cannot see;

15 They have ears, but cannot hear,

16 nor is the breath in their mouths.

17 Those who fashion them, all who trust in them, shall become like them.

18 O house of Israel, bless God; O house of Aaron, bless God;

19 O house of Levi, bless God; you who fear God, bless God.

20 Blessed is God from Zion, God who dwells in Jerusalem. Halleluyah.

PSALM 136

1 Praise God; for God is good, God's steadfast love is eternal.

2 Praise the God of Gods, God's e steadfast love is eternal.

3 Praise God of Gods, God's steadfast love is eternal;

4 Who alone works great marvels, God's steadfast love is eternal;

5 Who made the Heavens with wisdom, God's steadfast love is eternal;

6 Who spread the earth over the water, God's steadfast love is eternal;

7 Who made the great lights, God's steadfast love is eternal;

8 The sun to dominate the day, God's steadfast love is eternal;

9 The moon and the stars to dominate the night, God's steadfast love is eternal;

10 Who struck Egypt through their first-born, God's steadfast love is eternal;

11 and brought Israel out of their midst, God's steadfast love is eternal;

12 with a strong hand and outstretched arm, God's steadfast love is eternal;

13 Who split apart the Sea of Reeds, God's steadfast love is eternal;

14 and made Israel pass through it, God's steadfast love is eternal;

15 Who hurled Pharaoh and his army into The Sea of Reeds, God's steadfast love is eternal;

16 Who led God's people through the wilderness, God's steadfast love is eternal;

17 Who struck down great kings, God's steadfast love is eternal;

18 and slew mighty kings—God's steadfast love is eternal;

19 Sihon, king of the Amorites, God's steadfast love is eternal;

20 Og, king of Bashan—God's steadfast love is eternal;

21 and gave their land as a heritage, God's steadfast love is eternal;

22 a heritage to God's servant Israel, God's steadfast love is eternal;

23 Who took note of us in our degradation, God's steadfast love is eternal;

24 and rescued us from our enemies, God's steadfast love is eternal;

25 Who gives food to all flesh, God's steadfast love is eternal.

26 Praise The God of heaven, God's steadfast love is eternal.

The Great Hallel

When we confront Psalms 135 and 136, it is best to buckle our mind's seatbelt because it is a wild ride. So much lays beneath the surface; the twists and turns keep coming at us.

To understand the theme of these two Psalms, it helps to know that Jewish history renamed them The Great Hallel. *Hallel* means *praise* and is part of the phrase *Halleluyah*, or *praise God*. Indeed, these two Psalms are the gold standard of high praise for God with an exceptionally high number of praise-phrases embedded within them. There are two theories why Psalms 135 and 136 are called The Great Hallel. The first theory is because of that impressive number of praise-phrases. The other thought is because these Psalms praise God for the creation of the world and for the salvation of the Israelite People through the Exodus from Egypt. From the world view of Jewish history, the two events supremely worthy of great praise of God is the creation of the world and the salvation of the Israelite nation. And so we inherit The Great Hallel with its plethora of praises.

There is a subtext to all this praise. Our Psalms set up a comparison, even a contest, between the one true God and the idols worshipped by Israel's pagan neighbors. With each example of God's power and presence, there is praise offered.

> *The idols of the nations are silver and gold, the*
> *work of men's hands.*
> *They have mouths, but cannot speak; They have*
> *eyes, but cannot see;*

They have ears, but cannot hear,
nor is the breath in their mouths.

But for the God who created the universe and split the Red Sea, praise God. Halleluyah.

As literature, Psalms 135 and 136 are fascinating constructs. Psalms 135 and 136 present God's presence in history in chronological order: the world's creation, freeing the People Israel from Egyptian bondage, Israelite encounters on their journey through the Sinai Desert, and their safe passage to the Promised Land. Not only do we experience this rendering of God's miracles in history, but we also experience them twice!

In their own poetic ways, both Psalms recount God's manifest acts, and in several instances both Psalms rely on very similar language. Both are written as call and response pieces, with a prayer leader's part and a congregational response—and Psalm 136 is the only Psalm to do so in every verse. And we find that both Psalms rely on a catchphrase to praise God: in Psalm 135, we find *halleluyah* and *barkhu*, or *bless*; in Psalm 136, it reads, *God's steadfast love is eternal.*

Of additional literary interest is the realization that just about every verse in these Psalms has a parallel verse found elsewhere in the Bible, most in the Torah or in other Psalms. Because of all this, our two Psalms are considered to be one thematic unit and together are worthy of being called The Great Hallel.

A Numbers Game
Numbers play an interesting role in our Psalms. Psalm 135 opens with a four-fold repetition of *halleluyah* and it ends with a four-fold reference to *barkhu*. Three verses are repeated almost word for word in both Psalms. And in Psalm

136 the phrase *God's steadfast love is eternal* is a response to all twenty-six verses. Rabbis over the millennia had fun with this. They noted there were twenty-six generations from Adam to Mt. Sinai. They also noted that in Jewish mystical numerology known as Gematria, the central name of God—Y/H/V/H—is equal to twenty-six. All this provided the rabbis with opportunity to spin fanciful lessons.

Singing for the Rain

Water is another theme that runs through our Psalms. In Psalm 135 the seas are referenced in verse 6 and the rain in verse 7. In Psalm 136, verse 6, we find the waters that God spread out over the earth during the week of Creation, while verse 14 speaks of the splitting of the Red Sea. In ancient times, it was a custom to fast as a means of beseeching God to end a drought. The Talmud[1] tells us that if their fast was successful and the rains fell, these two Psalms were recited in celebration and praise.

SOUL STEPS

CIRCLES OF GRATITUDE

For all that God has done for the world—the wonders and beauties of creation—and for all that God has done for the people Israel (enumerated above), Psalms 135 and 136 call on us to bring forth an attitude of gratitude. Consider your world as a series of concentric circles, perhaps country, community, circles of friends, family. What gratitude do you hold for each circle? In the spirit of these Psalms, identify one word that captures your sense of gratitude or praise. Close your eyes and softly chant that word as you think about each circle in your world and the gratitude you hold for them.

[1] Mishnah Taanit 3:9

SUSTENANCE, LIFE, FREEDOM

Psalm 136 is represented in three prominent pieces of Jewish liturgy:

- The daily Jewish morning service begins with a series of blessings of appreciation. This Psalm's sixth verse—*Who spread the earth over the water*—is one of them, acknowledging that our ability to exist requires that there be dry land distinct from the oceans.
- Verse 25 forms the central theme of the first paragraph of *Birkhat Hamazon, the* grace after meals. In fact, this verse may have constituted an early version of the grace after meals.
- And in its entirety, Psalm 136 is found in the Passover Haggadah and is recited at each *Seder.*
- When taken together, these three liturgical experiences reflect sustenance, existence (life), and freedom. When you consider the sustenance you are blessed with, the freedom you experience, and your very existence, what is worthy of pronouncing Halleluyah?

THE PSALMS: FIVE BOOKS IN ONE

According to Jewish tradition, the "one" book of Psalms is made up of five distinct sub-books. They are:

Book One   Psalms 1-41
Book Two   Psalms 42-72
Book Three   Psalms 73-89
Book Four   Psalms 90-106
Book Five   Psalms 107-150

Bible scholars wonder why this is so. A leading thought is that the Psalms evolved as a collection over time with new material being added onto it. There is an important word to know in order to understand these five sub-divisions. That word is *doxology*, which is a liturgical composition that praises God.

We find a truly fascinating phenomenon within these five sub-books.

Books 1-4 end with a doxology that is almost exactly the same in each case.

Here are the last verses of the first four books. Note how similar they are.

Book One, Psalm 41:14

> *Blessed is the God of Israel, from eternity*
> *   to eternity.*
> *Amen and amen.*

Book Two, Psalm 72:18-20

> *Blessed is the God of Israel,*
> *Who alone does wondrous things;*
> *Blessed is God's name forever,*
> *And let God's glory fill the whole world.*
> *Amen and amen.*
> *End of the prayers of David, son of Jesse.*

Book Three, Psalm 89:53

> *Blessed is God to eternity. Amen and amen.*

Book Four, Psalm 106:48

> *Blessed is the God of Israel, from eternity to eternity.*
> *Let all the people say Amen. Halleluyah.*

Does Book 5 end with a similar verse? Actually Psalm 150, the very last Psalm, is entirely a doxology. In six short verses it contains thirteen variations of the word *halleluyah ("praise God")*, and calls on all living things to use nine different musical instruments to praise God. A truly fitting end to all five sub-books in the collection.

Afterword

THIS IS JUST THE BEGINNING

You've arrived at the end of this book. And yet, it is really just the beginning. The beauty of the Psalms is their ability to impact us in many different ways, depending on our mindset and how we are experiencing life at a given moment in time.

This is a lesson I learned in my last year of rabbinical school, when my teacher Rabbi Simon Greenberg, of blessed memory, offered a seminar formulating one's philosophy of life. Each week, we grappled with nuanced aspects of theology and philosophy. At the end of the course, each student wrote a thesis paper, formulating our personal worldviews and values to live by. On the last day, we told Rabbi Greenberg how meaningful his class had been to us and asked if he would continue teaching us the following semester. He said he would . . . but only if we agreed to reflect upon, reconsider, and revise our worldviews.

His point was that as we move through this world in time and place, our values and perspectives should grow and change. He asked us to continue thinking about our viewpoints and our values, and to always be open to new insights.

So, too, does our relationship with the Psalms evolve depending on how and what we are experiencing in life. You've journeyed through the Psalms as presented in these pages. Hopefully you've learned about the context, construct, and inner workings of the Psalms. You've engaged with specific Psalms; studied their themes and experienced their pathos. Through the Soul Steps you've brought the messages of the Psalms into your daily life. You've been mindful of the ways they hold meaning for you. They have, perhaps, stirred your soul and inspired reflection.

I invite you to engage with these selected Psalms and the many others not included in this volume. From time to time, pick a Psalm and ask yourself, how does this make me feel? Are there values represented that resonate? How might I include those values in my life?

Or perhaps the Psalm discomforts you. Identify why that is so. If it has a worldview that is not your own, use that discomfort to clarify what it is you believe. If you are so motivated, investigate the history of that Psalm so that you might gain better insight into the poet's motivation for crafting it. If you are experiencing a peak life moment, look to the charts that follow for suggested Psalms that might speak to your life experience.

The Psalms are a gift to the heart and soul. May you find joy, excitement, comfort, and support as you unwrap that gift. And each time you revisit the Psalms may they be for you, as they are for me, the gift that keeps on giving.

Appendix A

PSALMS FOR LIFE'S MOMENTS BY TOPIC

THEME	EXPERIENCE	PSALM
WHEN LIFE IS CHALLENGING	Fighting an enemy within, such as addiction recovery or emotional turmoil	3 5 7 9:14 13 18 25 34 55:17–19 & 23 61 69 77 121 123 141 143
	Confronting good and evil	5 37 41 94 109

WHEN LIFE IS CHALLENGING (CONT.)	Confronting interpersonal strife	12:3–4 15 133
	Grappling with justice & injustice	7 58 75 82 109 146:5–10
CELEBRATING LIFE'S BOUNTIES	Appreciating life's bounties, identifying values for a good life	4:8 34:13–15 67:7 85:12–13 112 147
	Feeling uplifted in life	3 10:17–18 111 113
PRAISEWORTHY ROLE MODELS	Celebrating a person of faith	37 40 62 101 112
	Celebrating a righteous person	1 15 34:13–15 92:13–15 97:11–12 101 112

PRAISEWORTHY ROLE MODELS (CONT.)	For a humble person, in praise of humility	30 86 131
	Celebrating music, for a musician	57:8–12 81 98 100:1–2 149, 150
OTHER	Making a pilgrimage to Israel, Jerusalem	48 84 122 125 126 137 147
	Ecumenical gatherings	96 100:1 133 150:6
	Celebrating learning, educational accomplishment, celebrating Torah	19:8–9 & 15 78:5–7 119 132:12
	A safe journey	91:10–12 121
OF PARTICULAR INTEREST TO CLERGY	"The meek shall inherit the earth"	37:11
	For Rosh Hashanah	48

OF PARTICULAR INTEREST TO CLERGY (CONT.)	The arc of Biblical Jewish history and the importance of tradition	79
	The tormented history of Jerusalem	80
	A parallel to the 13 Attributes	86:16
	Celebrating a victory for the Jewish people	98
	An enhancement for Rosh Hashana	100
	A reading for fast days	103
	For liminal calendar moments, such as new seasons and new beginnings	105
	For Passover	114
	Part of Havdalah	116:13
	Expression of collective hope by and for the Jewish people	131:3
	How good it is for brethren to sit together	133:1
	Celebrating those who work on behalf of the synagogue	134
	Celebrating a communal new beginning	149:1

Appendix B

PSALMS FOR LIFE'S MOMENTS IN NUMERIC ORDER

PSALM	EXPERIENCE
1	Celebrating a righteous person
2	Expressing faith in God
3	• Feeling besieged • Fighting an enemy within, addiction recovery • During times of recovery and emotional turmoil • Feeling uplifted in life
4	• Celebrating love (4:8) • When pleading with God • For appreciating life's bounties, Values for a good life (4:8)
5	• Feeling abandoned, Needing God to be near (5:2–4) • Fighting an enemy within, addiction recovery, emotional turmoil • Feeling besieged • Confronting good and evil
6	Confronting illness
7	• Feeling besieged • Fighting an enemy within, addiction recovery, emotional turmoil • On justice and injustice

8	• Appreciating the natural world and creation (8:4 & 10) • Feeling God's closeness • Reflecting on God's goodness
9	• Feeling besieged • Fighting an enemy within, addiction recovery, emotional turmoil (9:14)
10	• Feeling abandoned, Needing God to be near • Feeling uplifted in life (10:17–18)
11	• Expressing faith in God • For finding one's faith again
12	Confronting interpersonal strife (12:3–4)
13	• Feeling distant from God • Needing to lash out at God • Expressing faith in God • For finding one's faith again • Fighting an enemy within, addiction recovery, emotional turmoil
14	Expressing faith in God
15	• Celebrating a righteous person • Confronting interpersonal strife
16	• Expressing faith in God • For finding one's faith again
17	For a journey of repentance or soul cleansing
18	• Following a natural disaster (18:8ff) • Feeling besieged (18:33ff) • Needing or celebrating salvation • Fighting an enemy within, addiction recovery, emotional turmoil

19	• Appreciating the natural world and creation (19:2–7) • Celebrating learning, educational accomplishment, celebrating Torah (19:8–9, 15)
20	• Celebrating a birthday or anniversary • Honoring a good person (20:5–7) • Celebrating love (20:5) • Confronting illness • At a time of physical or spiritual distress
21	Feeling besieged
22	• Feeling distant from God • Needing to lash out at God • At a time of physical or spiritual distress • Needing or celebrating salvation
23	While reflecting on mortality/aging/mourning
24	• Appreciating the natural world and creation • Expressing faith in God, Finding one's faith again
25	• For a journey of repentance or soul cleansing • Fighting an enemy within, addiction recovery, emotional turmoil
26	For a journey of repentance or soul cleansing
27	• Confronting illness (27:13–14) • At a time of physical or spiritual distress • Feeling besieged • Needing or celebrating salvation
28	• Expressing faith in God • For finding one's faith again (28:6–9) • Experiencing calm after chaos • Needing or celebrating salvation

29	• Appreciating the natural world • Following a natural disaster, such as an earthquake
30	• For a humble person, in praise of humility • Confronting illness • Needing or celebrating salvation
31	• Celebrating a birthday or anniversary • Honoring a good person (31:25) • Feeling besieged
32	For a journey of repentance or soul cleansing
33	Appreciating the natural world and creation (33:6–8)
34	• Celebrating a righteous person (34:13–15) • Celebrating a birthday or anniversary • Fighting an enemy within, addiction recovery, emotional turmoil • Appreciating life's bounties, Values for a good life (34:13–15)
35	Feeling besieged
36	• Celebrating a birthday or anniversary • Honoring a good person (36:10–11) • Celebrating love (36:10–11)
37	• Celebrating a person of faith • Confronting good and evil
38	Feeling abandoned, Needing God to be near (38:16, 22, 23)
39	• Reflecting on mortality, aging, mourning • For a journey of repentance or soul cleansing

40	• Celebrating a person of faith • Celebrating a birthday, anniversary, honoring a good person • Praising one who works for the community (40:8-12)
41	Confronting good and evil
42	Feeling abandoned, Needing God to be near
43	• Feeling abandoned, Needing God to be near • Expressing faith in God, Finding one's faith again (43:3-5)
44	Feeling besieged
45	• Celebrating a birthday or anniversary, honoring a good person • On building a legacy (45:18) • Celebrating love
46	Following a natural disaster, such as an earthquake
47	• Feeling God's closeness • Expressing faith in God
48	For a pilgrimage to Israel/Jerusalem
49	• Expressing faith in God, Finding one's faith again • Needing or celebrating salvation
50	Reflecting on God's goodness (50:14)
51	For a journey of repentance or soul cleansing
52	Expressing faith in God
53	Expressing faith in God
54	• Pleading with God • Feeling besieged

55	• Feeling besieged • Needing or celebrating salvation • Fighting an enemy within, addiction recovery, emotional turmoil (55:17–19, 23)
56	Feeling besieged
57	• Celebrating music, for a musician (57:8–12) • Fighting an enemy within, addiction recovery, emotional turmoil (55:17–19, 23) • Needing or celebrating salvation
58	On justice and injustice
59	• Experiencing calm after chaos (59:17–18) • Feeling besieged
60	• Feeling distant from God • Needing to lash out at God • Feeling abandoned and needing God to be near
61	• Expressing faith in God; finding one's faith again • Fighting an enemy within, addiction recovery, emotional turmoil • Needing or celebrating salvation
62	• Celebrating a person of faith • Expressing faith in God, Finding one's faith again
63	Expressing faith in God; finding one's faith again
64	• Pleading with God • Feeling besieged
65	• Appreciating the natural world and creation • Confronting a drought
66	Reflecting on God's goodness
67	• Appreciating the natural world and creation (67:7) • Appreciating life's bounties, Values for a good life (67:7)

68	• Expressing faith in God, Finding one's faith again • Reflecting on God's goodness • At a time of communal calamity
69	• At a time of physical or spiritual distress • Fighting an enemy within, addiction recovery, emotional turmoil
70	Feeling abandoned or needing God to be near
71	• Reflecting on mortality, aging, mourning (especially 71:9) • Feeling God's closeness • Expressing faith in God, Finding one's faith again
72	• On justice and injustice • Reflecting on God's goodness (72:17–19)
73	Feeling God's closeness (23–28)
74	At a time of communal calamity
75	On justice and injustice
76	• Needing or celebrating salvation • On justice (76:9–10)
77	Fighting an enemy within, addiction recovery, emotional turmoil
78	Celebrating learning, educational accomplishment, celebrating Torah (78:5–7)
79	• At a time of communal calamity • Pleading with God • Feeling abandoned or needing God to be near
80	At a time of communal calamity
81	Celebrating music, for a musician
82	On justice and injustice
83	• Needing God to be near • On justice and injustice

84	Pilgrimage to Israel/Jerusalem
85	• Feeling besieged • Needing or celebrating salvation • Appreciating life's bounties, Values for a good life (85:12–13)
86	• For a humble person, in praise of humility • Expressing faith in God, Finding one's faith again • Needing or celebrating salvation
87	For a pilgrimage to Jerusalem
88	• Feeling abandoned, Needing God to be near • At a time of physical or spiritual distress
89	Expressing faith in God, Finding one's faith again
90	• Celebrating a birthday or anniversary • Honoring a good person (90:12 on wisdom) • Reflecting on mortality, aging, mourning
91	• Celebrating a birthday or anniversary • Honoring a good person (91:10–12) • Needing or celebrating salvation • For a safe journey (91:10–12)
92	Celebrating a righteous person (92:13–15)
93	Appreciating the natural world and creation
94	• Reflecting on God's goodness (94:18–19, 22) • Confronting good and evil
95	Expressing faith in God, Finding one's faith again
96	Ecumenical gatherings
97	Celebrating a righteous person (97:11–12)
98	• Celebrating music, for a musician • Celebrating a birthday or anniversary • Honoring a good person

99	• The arc of Biblical Jewish history • On justice and injustice • Expressing faith in God
100	• Celebrating music, for a musician (100:1–2) • Ecumenical gatherings (100:1)
101	• Celebrating a person of faith • Celebrating a righteous person
102	Needing or celebrating salvation
103	• Confronting illness • For a journey of repentance or soul cleansing
104	• Appreciating the natural world and creation • Celebrating new life, birth, Brit Milah, Simhat Bat, celebrating a child
105	• Expressing faith in God, Finding one's faith again • Reflecting on God's goodness
106	For a journey of repentance or soul cleansing (106:1–9)
107	• Reflecting on God's goodness • Feeling God's closeness • Needing or celebrating salvation
108	Needing or celebrating salvation
109	• Feeling besieged • Confronting good and evil • On justice and injustice
110	• On justice and injustice • Feeling besieged
111	• Expressing faith in God, Finding one's faith again • Reflecting on God's goodness • Feeling uplifted in life

112	• Celebrating a person of faith • Celebrating a righteous person • Appreciating life's bounties, Values for a good life
113	• Expressing faith in God, Finding one's faith again • Feeling uplifted in life
114	Needing or celebrating salvation
115	• Celebrating a birthday, anniversary, honoring a good person • 115:14–15 a simple beautiful wish • Celebrating love (115:14–15)
116	• Feeling God's closeness (God answers prayers) • Needing or celebrating salvation
117	• Feeling God's closeness • Reflecting on God's goodness
118	• Reflecting on God's goodness (118:23–24) • Feeling besieged • For a journey of repentance or soul cleansing (118:19–21)
119	• Celebrating a birthday, anniversary, honoring a good person • Celebrating learning, educational accomplishment, celebrating Torah
120	• Feeling besieged • Feeling God's closeness
121	• Fighting an enemy within, addiction recovery, emotional turmoil • For a safe journey
122	Pilgrimage to Israel/Jerusalem
123	Fighting an enemy within, addiction recovery, emotional turmoil

124	• Feeling besieged • Feeling God's closeness
125	Pilgrimage to Israel/Jerusalem
126	Pilgrimage to Israel/Jerusalem
127	• Celebrating new life, birth, *Brit Milah*, *Simhat Bat*, celebrating a child (127:3) • At a time of celebration (birthday, anniversary, honoring a good person) (127:7–8)
128	• Celebrating new life, birth, Brit Milah, Simhat Bat, celebrating a child • At a time of celebration (birthday, anniversary, honoring a good person)
129	• Feeling besieged • Feeling God's closeness
130	For a journey of repentance or soul cleansing
131	For a humble person, in praise of humility
132	Celebrating learning, educational accomplishment, celebrating Torah (132:12)
133	• Confronting interpersonal strife • Ecumenical gatherings
134	Ecumenical gatherings
135	Celebrating rainfall
136	• Appreciating the natural world and creation • Expressing faith in God, Finding one's faith again • Reflecting on God's goodness
137	Pilgrimage to Israel/Jerusalem
138	Needing or celebrating salvation (138:8)
139	• Expressing Faith in God • Needing or celebrating salvation

140	• Feeling besieged • Confronting good and evil • Expressing faith in God
141	Fighting an enemy within, addiction recovery, emotional turmoil
142	Feeling abandoned, Needing God to be near
143	Fighting an enemy within, addiction recovery, emotional turmoil
144	Needing or celebrating salvation
145	• Appreciating the natural world and creation (145:5) • Expressing faith in God, Finding one's faith again
146	On justice and injustice (146:-5-10)
147	• Celebrating rainfall (147:8) • Pilgrimage to Israel • Appreciating life's bounties, Values for a good life
148	• Appreciating the natural world and creation • Expressing faith in God, Finding one's faith again
149	Celebrating music, for a musician
150	• Celebrating music, for a musician • Ecumenical gatherings (150:6)

ACKNOWLEDGMENTS

It truly does take a village to produce a book. My village included these wonderful folks.

I so appreciate that friends and colleagues took the time to read the manuscript and offer honest feedback. Their positive feedback supported me and their critiques and suggestions were exceedingly helpful. They found typos, identified confusing sentences, and offered really great creative ideas. For this I thank Rabbi Daniel Pressman, Rabbi Amy Eilberg, Rabbi Steven Razin, David Fishman, Michal Strutin, and Eric Rosenblum.

I need to single out Rabbi Steven Razin for his support, cheerleading, and editorial excellence. We were roommates in college and lifelong friends ever since. Who knew you were such a superb copy editor? You called or texted regularly to encourage my progress and you lovingly asked to preview each new element I finished. And each time I sent you a new piece of writing, you sent it back with excellent suggestions and ideas. Most of those found their way into the book and it is profoundly better because of you.

I appreciate the graciousness shown me by Rabbi Jack Riemer. You agreed to read the manuscript and offered encouragement to bring this book into the public sphere.

Michal Strutin is a cherished friend and incredible author (do yourself a favor and check out her many books – you are in for a treat!). Because of your own experience writing books and bringing them to light, you were a fountain of helpful, practical, and insightful information. Many a Shabbat we discussed the difficult journey of book-making. You shared your vast wisdom and graciously encouraged my own journey as an author.

With pride and joy I turned to my personal graphic designer and favorite first son, Elie Berkowitz. You shared your skills and your designer's eye in crafting the book's graphics and the wonderful cover design. Eye pourus b'momdu.

This book was a hot mess until the very excellent Laura Mazar spoke truth to me. With the professionalism that you bring to your career as a book editor and author's agent, early on you spoke this truth. "I feel like this is a confusing two books in one. Part of it reads like a scholarly, academic textbook; and part of it reads like a very accessible mindfulness journey through the Psalms. I think you need to pick one and personally, I hope it is the mindfulness path." With that you gave me the golden key that unlocked the book I really wanted to write (but didn't have the clarity to know it). I started over and here we are. And then you shepherded the manuscript and me through the publishing process, even volunteering to be the book's editor. Thanks, Cousin. You are the best!

Mindy, wife and partner: together we bounce through life, finding lots and lots of things to laugh about. You were kind enough to not raise an eyebrow (at least outwardly) when I said I wanted to write this book. You were supportive, complimentary, and offered a good critical eye on key pieces that are now better because of your discernment.

To all, thank you!

Light is sown for the righteous, joy for the upright. (Psalms 97:11)

May each of you be blessed with radiant light and joy.

ABOUT THE AUTHOR

Allan Berkowitz received his BA from the Hebrew University in Jerusalem and his rabbinic ordination from the Jewish Theological Seminary. He holds a Master's Degree in Education from Columbia University Teachers College.

Allan has focused his career on executive management in the nonprofit sector, including 17 years as the executive director of an award-winning San Francisco bay area environmental education nonprofit and most recently in community organizing in pursuit of social justice and equity.

Allan is the co-author of *Embracing the Covenant: Converts to Judaism Talk about Why & How* (Jewish Lights Publishing). He is the producer of numerous multimedia presentations and videos highlighting the powerful works of nonprofits. With a talent for making traditional texts come alive, his Torah study classes are highly popular. Allan lives in the San Francisco Bay Area.

www.ingramcontent.com/pod-product-compliance
Lightning Source LLC
Chambersburg PA
CBHW022011090426
42741CB00007B/981